Music Theory
The Foundation of Great Music

Sean Atkinson, PhD

THE
GREAT
COURSES®

MIX
Paper from
responsible sources
FSC® C011935

THE GREAT COURSES®

4840 Westfields Boulevard | Suite 500 | Chantilly, Virginia | 20151-2299
[PHONE] 1.800.832.2412 | [FAX] 703.378.3819 | [WEB] www.thegreatcourses.com

LEADERSHIP

PAUL SUIJK	President & CEO
BRUCE G. WILLIS	Chief Financial Officer
JOSEPH PECKL	SVP, Marketing
JASON SMIGEL	VP, Product Development
CALE PRITCHETT	VP, Marketing
MARK LEONARD	VP, Technology Services
DEBRA STORMS	VP, General Counsel
KEVIN MANZEL	Sr. Director, Content Development
ANDREAS BURGSTALLER	Sr. Director, Brand Marketing & Innovation
KEVIN BARNHILL	Director of Creative
GAIL GLEESON	Director, Business Operations & Planning

PRODUCTION TEAM

TOM KRZYWICKI	Producer
ELLIOT BLAIR SMITH	Content Developer
JULIET RILEY	Associate Producer
TRISA BARNHILL PETER DWYER	Graphic Artists
OWEN YOUNG	Managing Editor
ANDREW VOLPE KRISTEN WESTPHAL	Editors
CHARLES GRAHAM	Assistant Editor
ED SALTZMAN	Audio Engineer
GEORGE BOLDEN VALERIE WELCH	Camera Operators
PAUL SHEEHAN SHARON SOBEL	Production Assistants
ROBERTO DE MORAES	Director

PUBLICATIONS TEAM

FARHAD HOSSAIN	Publications Manager
MARTIN STEGER	Senior Copywriter
KATHRYN DAGLEY	Graphic Designer
JESSICA MULLINS	Proofreader
ERIKA ROBERTS	Publications Assistant
GINA DALFONZO	Fact-Checker
WILLIAM DOMANSKI	Transcript Editor

Sean Atkinson, PhD

Associate Professor of Music Theory
Texas Christian University

Sean Atkinson is an Associate Professor of Music Theory at the Texas Christian University School of Music, where he teaches courses on topics such as music theory, aural skills, and form and analysis. He also teaches graduate seminars on music analysis and musical meaning as well as a media studies class for the university's Honors College. Prior to joining the faculty at TCU, he taught in the Department of Music at The University of Texas at Arlington. He holds a BM in Music Theory and Trombone Performance from Furman University and earned MM and PhD degrees in Music Theory from Florida State University.

Professor Atkinson's research, which broadly addresses issues of musical meaning in multimedia contexts, has been published in journals such as *Music Theory Online, Indiana Theory Review,* the *Dutch Journal of Music Theory,* and *Popular Music.* He is also active in the growing field of video game music (ludomusicology) and has presented at the North American Conference on Video Game Music and the Music and the Moving Image Conference at New York University.

Professor Atkinson is a cofounder of No Quarters, an on-campus video game lab at TCU committed to the interdisciplinary research and teaching of video games. Housed in the library, the lab allows students and teachers to explore a growing number of games and consoles, including virtual reality.

Table of Contents

Introduction

Guides

Supplementary Material

Learning the Language of Music

Imagine listening to a favorite concerto, symphony, or song, and hearing something of interest to you. Then, imagine being able to read music. That will allow you to look up the interesting part of the music in the score and then discover what notes are being played or other aspects of the arrangement that make it special to you.

This course will teach you the basics of reading music. But even more than that, its goal is to teach you how to become literate in the language of music. Many people have the misconception that reading music is too hard or not necessary. They hear about famous musicians who never learned to read music and think, "Well, if they don't need to read music, why would I?"

It's true that many famous musicians, including Paul McCartney, never did learn how to read music. He and his fellow Beatles were successful at learning music by ear. But most professional musicians do read music. They find they have to. Possessing musical fluency unlocks a whole world of new possibility and discovery.

Musical fluency also entails a basic understanding of what makes music work. Most music we listen to—whether it is a Johann Sebastian Bach cantata from the early 1700s or a song you heard on the radio yesterday—follows a similar set of rules when it comes to things like musical phrasing and harmony. Knowing what notes are playing and how they fit into the musical texture will enrich your listening experience.

Outline of the Course

⬦ This course's journey begins with the music itself. Lesson 1's video involves an immersion into the musical world of Nikolai Rimsky-Korsakov's Russian Easter Overture. In the lessons that follow in the first part of the course, you will begin to learn the fundamentals of music. These are the basic building blocks of reading music, such as note reading and identifying major and minor keys.

⬦ After you learn about musical intervals, you will discover that the major and minor keys in music are all related to each other in what is commonly referred to as the circle of fifths.

⬦ Near the midpoint of the course, it introduces the old technique of counterpoint. You will learn how to compose your own music by following the same rules and guidelines taught to Western music's greatest composers.

⬦ In the second half of the course, you will apply your knowledge of music fundamentals and begin to develop a true sense of musical fluency. You will discover how harmony in tonal music works by learning the ins and outs of triads and seventh chords.

⬦ You'll also learn that harmonies in music tend to follow a specific pattern that is common to all kinds of different music, from classical to jazz to rock and roll. Additionally, the course reveals how music comes together in larger groups called phrases.

⬦ In the later lessons of the course, you will bring together everything you've learned so far. You will learn how to read lead sheets, a unique musical score that provides only minimal instructions, requiring a great deal of interpretation in performance. The final lesson in this course is a test involving Clara Schumann's beautiful piece Three Romances for Violin and Piano.

⬦ Both reading and understanding music are essential in developing a true fluency with music. By the conclusion of the course, you will walk away with the confidence to pick up a piece of music, read the notes on the page, and understand how the notes and everything else on the page contribute to the music you love.

The Russian Easter Overture

⬦ The video component of lesson 1 features a walkthrough of the Russian Easter Overture, incorporating a performance by the Texas Christian University Symphony Orchestra. The Russian Easter Overture was written in 1888 by Nikolai Rimsky-Korsakov, during the prime of his life.

⬦ Living in St. Petersburg, he was an architect of Russian nationalistic classical music, drawing on the Russian folk song tradition as well as complex harmonies, melodies, and rhythms. Phillip Huscher, a scholar in residence with the Chicago Symphony Orchestra, describes the Russian Easter Overture as "a vivid first-hand account of Easter morning service." It's a remarkable portrait of a holy day in the Russian Orthodox Church.

⬦ The piece transitions between several different sections, highlighting the range of emotions that accompany Easter celebrations. For a discussion of those sections guided by this course's instructor, refer to the video lesson.

*Go to page 111 to view the score for
Nikolai Rimsky-Korsakov's Russian Easter Overture.*

QUESTIONS TO CONSIDER

1 How does reading music enrich your experience of music?

2 What does it mean to be musically literate?

Staff, Clefs, and Notes

This lesson discusses how to identify pitch—that is, the frequency of a note that produces tones that are higher or lower than the notes around it. The lesson introduces the basics of the staff—a series of lines and spaces on the page—and clefs, which are symbols at the beginning of the staff that indicate which lines and spaces correspond to which notes on a written score. Fortunately, Western musical notation is quite good at laying out a clear map to follow toward pitch identification.

The Piano Keyboard

- The first seven letters of the alphabet—A, B, C, D, E, F, and G—are used to indicate pitch. Pitch can also be understood as the frequency, or vibration rate, of a sound wave.

- Looking at the piano keyboard, this concept becomes clearer. For instance, after starting with a white key that produces the note A and moving up, the next white key is a B, then a C, and so on up to G. After G—the seventh and final letter of the alphabet that we are going to adapt to musical notation—we start over with A again.

- That A is now an octave—or eight pitches—higher than the first A. Any pitches that have the same name will sound similar, only higher or lower.

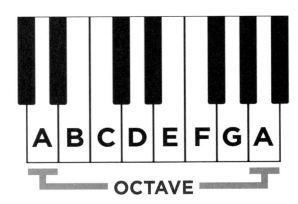

This lesson uses the example of a quarter note to show how notes are positioned on the staff. The quarter note is an oval-shaped dot. Attached to the side is a long line, which is called a stem. The pitch itself is indicated solely by where the note head is placed on the staff.

The Basics of the Staff

- On a five-line staff of modern notation, each line—and each space—indicates a different pitch. Any note placed on a line or space tells the performer which pitch to play, from A to G.

- An understanding of clefs—the large symbols at the beginning of every staff—is necessary to know which line corresponds to which pitch. Clefs let you know where the pitches are in the upper or lower register.

- There are a number of different clefs that can be used, each one suited to different instruments depending on how high or low that instrument plays—that is, the range of the instrument. Two clefs are seen most of the time, however: the treble clef and the bass clef.

The Treble Clef

The treble clef is primarily used by instruments with a higher range, such as a typical female's voice, flutes, violins, and the right-hand part on piano. Though the symbol resembles an elaborate letter S, the treble clef is sometimes called a G-clef because the swirling part in the middle indicates the note G.

The swirl surrounds the second line from the bottom of the five-line staff, and that line corresponds with the pitch G. As a hint to get started, when you see the treble clef, you'll immediately know where the note G is. Finding the other notes is simply a matter of running through the musical alphabet.

Recalling that G is the seventh and final letter that music borrows from the alphabet, you'll realize that moving up from G to the space above it means starting the alphabet over again at A. The next line above the A is B. The next space is C. The next line is D. The top space is E. And the top line of the staff is F. Alternatively, moving down, the space below G is F. And the bottom line of the staff is E.

Becoming familiar with the names of the pitches takes a little bit of practice. You want to be able to recognize the notes on the fly rather than needing to find G, and then moving up or down from there. But there are a few mnemonic devices—or memory clues—that can help.

To remember the lines from bottom to top of the treble clef staff—E-G-B-D-F—you can think of this phrase: "Every Great Book Delivers Fun." Alternatively, think of this one: "Elephants Get Bored Dancing Fast." You can also make up your own. The sillier it is, the more likely you will be to remember it.

For the spaces of the treble clef staff, the combination of F-A-C-E conveniently spells the word *face*. That is an easy way to remember the notes of the staff lying within the spaces.

The Bass Clef

The bass clef is used for instruments with a lower range, such as a typical male voice and the cello and trombone. It's sometimes referred to as an F-clef because the two dots on the right of the clef bookend the line corresponding to an F pitch. From bottom to top, the lines of the bass clef are G-B-D-F-A. The spaces are A-C-E-G.

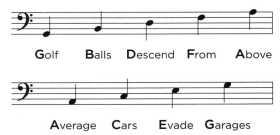

Again, memorable mnemonics can help. For the lines, you might say, "Goofy Bubbles Definitely Fall Apart," or "Golf Balls Descend From Above," or whatever you want to come up with. For the spaces, try saying, "All Cactus Eventually Grow," or "Average Cars Evade Garages," or your own.

Golf   Balls   Descend   From   Above

Average   Cars   Evade   Garages

G A B C D E F G A

Multiple Notes and Ledger Lines

In piano music, it is common for the left-hand part to feature multiple notes appearing at the same time. This is common because pianists are able to use each finger to play many notes simultaneously.

Another tricky factor is that some notes float above the staff on their own small lines. These are called ledger lines. Think of them like a step stool. They help to extend the staff both above and below the normal five-line staff. They are useful for indicating a note just above or below the staff.

To identify a note on a ledger line, imagine the staff lines continue past the top space. If the top space is B, then the first ledger line above it is a C. The space above that is D. The second ledger line is E. Therefore, those first notes in the bass clef are C and E.

Sometimes, the clef changes. This is a way for the composer to avoid having to use a bunch of ledger lines.

E F G A B C D E F G A B C D E F G A B C

Reading music with ledger lines is harder than reading music in the staff, even for professional musicians.

QUESTIONS TO CONSIDER

1 How does the musical staff help to convey the names of notes when reading music?

2 Why are different clefs needed for different instruments?

EXERCISE: Note-Reading

Identify each note.

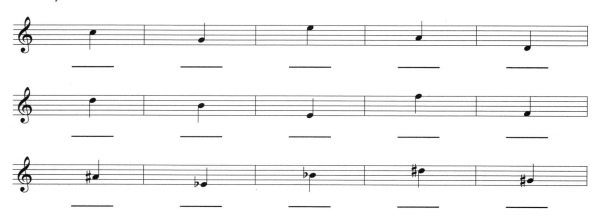

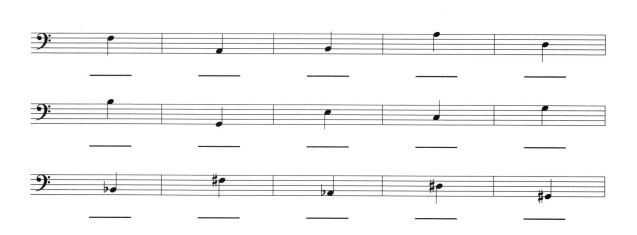

Answers for Note-Reading Exercise

Identify each note.

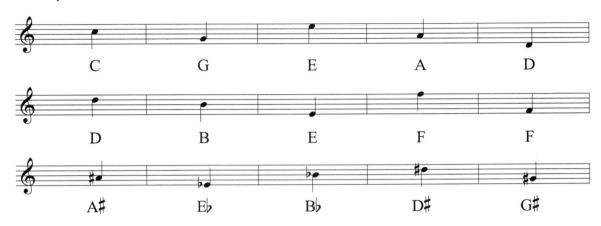

C   G   E   A   D

D   B   E   F   F

A♯   E♭   B♭   D♯   G♯

F   A   B   A   D

B   G   E   C   G

B♭   F♯   A♭   D♯   G♯

Major Scales: Notes in Context

Scales are one of the basic units on which music is built. The relationship between the pitches in a scale sets up an ordered system that can be used to create tension and release, driving the music forward. This lesson introduces certain scales and some of the various ways the notes in the scales interact.

Distances between Notes: Half Steps

⋄ The distance between notes is called an interval. Intervals can be small, like the distance on the piano from one key to the very next one. They can also be big, like the octave distance between two As. The two smallest intervals in Western music are the half step and the whole step.

⋄ Any two notes that are immediate neighbors on the piano keyboard, including the black keys, are also separated by a half step. An example would be the keys for F and F-sharp.

⋄ Between the two piano keys for the notes of B and C, there is no black key. It, too, is a half step. The same thing happens between E and F. Many people become confused by this, but it's simply a matter of committing to memory the two points on a keyboard where there is only a half-note interval.

You'll always find it between the B and C and between an E and F.

⋄ Another important consideration is what happens when you move down a half step. Starting at pitch D, for instance, moving down a half step will cause you to land on a black key. Moving up a half step from C will make you arrive at the same note.

⋄ This note can have two different names: C-sharp and D-flat. In musical notation, a sharp raises the pitch of a note by a half step. A flat lowers the pitch of a note by a half step.

⋄ Therefore, this same note may have two different names depending on the application of the note in a given situation. In fact, all keys on the piano have potentially two names. This is a feature of notation known as enharmonics.

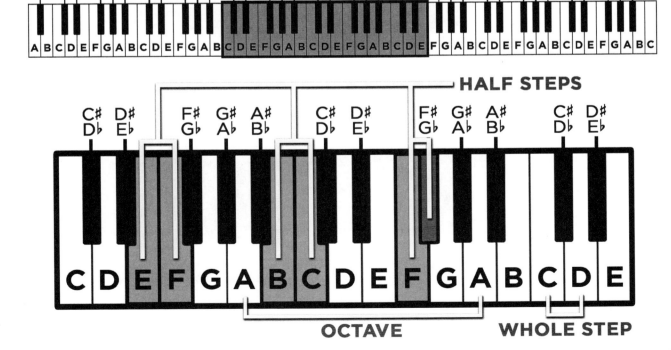

Distances between Notes: Whole Steps

◇ One way to think of whole steps is as two half steps put together. For example, starting from C, moving a whole step above C means skipping over C-sharp and landing on D. From there, you can move another whole step to E.

◇ Note that there is no piano key—no pitch—between E and F. Therefore, moving up a whole step from E skips the F and lands on F-sharp. You can move down by whole step, too. For instance, it is possible to move from F-sharp down to E, then to D and back to C.

Building Scales

◇ There are numerous types of scales in music. In the tonal music most common to Western audiences, major or minor scales are predominant. But there are other ways to organize pitches, including by combining half steps and whole steps in a number of different arrangements. Examples of those include chromatic, whole tone, and pentatonic scales.

◇ In the case of C major, you use only the white keys on the piano. For notational purposes, the music reflects no sharps or flats. It's easy to play and write out, and it's a great reference if you ever get confused about where the next whole step or half step is located.

◇ This lesson, however, focuses on major scales. All major scales follow the identical pattern of intervals. That is, they follow the same formula of half steps and whole steps, differing only on which note you start from.

C MAJOR SCALE

◇ Take the C major scale as an example. Starting on C, the scale moves by a whole step and then another whole step, followed by a half step, then three more whole steps. It ends on a half step to arrive back on a C. That pattern is the basis of every major scale.

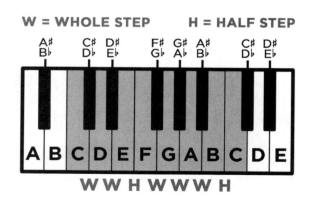

Scale Terminology

In addition to a note name, every note in a scale also has a functional name. This name describes the role of that note based on its position in the scale. Where a note is located within a scale dictates how that note is used in a piece of music. For example, even though a C major scale and an F major scale have different notes, the fifth note of each scale will follow the same tendencies when heard in the context of that scale.

The first note of the scale is called the tonic. It is ultimately where the scale concludes at the top end. You can think of the tonic as the place where the music also strives to resolve to. Hearing the tonic note of a scale usually feels like a place to rest. It sounds like an expression that is complete.

The next-most-important note is the fifth note of the scale. This one is called the dominant. The dominant is the unstable foil to tonic's restfulness. It's the place a piece will likely move toward on its way to get back to tonic.

Another note in the scale with an uneasiness about it is the leading tone—that is, the seventh note of the scale. Being a half step away from tonic, it wants to lead strongly back to the tonic, hence the name.

Immediately below the dominant is the fourth note of the scale, which is called the subdominant. The subdominant will sometimes help bridge the space between tonic and dominant. At other times, the musician will want to resolve the subdominant down to the third note of the scale. This is a half step.

In music theory, the third note is called the mediant because of its middle position between tonic and dominant. The mediant is a relatively stable note with no strong tendencies to move in one direction or another. Like the tonic, it is a jumping-off point to anywhere.

The sixth note of the scale is called the submediant. Like the mediant, the submediant has no strong tendency to move in any particular way.

The last note to discuss is the second degree of the scale, known as the supertonic. Despite its heroic-sounding moniker, the supertonic is not a stronger version of the tonic but simply the note above it. It will often resolve down to tonic, but it can just as easily move up to the mediant.

1	=	TONIC
2	=	SUPERTONIC
3	=	MEDIANT
4	=	SUBDOMINANT
5	=	DOMINANT
6	=	SUBMEDIANT
7	=	LEADING TONE
8	=	TONIC

QUESTIONS TO CONSIDER

1 What role do scales play in music?

2 Why is the pattern of whole steps and half steps in a major scale important?

EXERCISE: Scale Practice

Write out the notes of each scale.

C Major

B♭ Major

F Major

A Major

G Major

Add accidentals to the following notes to create major scales.

D Major

G Major

F Major

A Major

E Major

Answers for Scale Practice Exercise

Write out the notes of each scale.

Add accidentals to the following notes to create major scales.

Intervals: Distance between Notes

After the ability to read notes, knowing the intervals between notes is the most important part of learning to read music. The motion in a piece of music constantly creates new intervals that we can see and hear in the melody. Intervals are a way of talking about how the music moves.

Melody is the succession of notes that create the tune of a piece of music. Harmony is the support for the melody that occurs when two or more notes are played at the same time. These two fundamental aspects of music are both best described by the intervals between notes.

Interval Size

◇ Imagine that you are starting at middle C and want to know and describe the interval from C to E. You can simply count the number of steps it takes to get there in the C major scale. Starting with C as step 1, you would move through D as step 2 and arrive on E as step 3. Because there are three steps, this interval is a third.

◇ You can play interval as a melody— that is, as successive notes that might be part of a longer tune. Alternatively, you can play it as a harmony, sounding the notes at the same time. No matter how these notes are heard, the interval's size remains a third.

◇ The same counting procedure can be used to describe other intervals as well. For instance, moving from C to G encompasses C, D, E, F, and G—an interval called a fifth. Moving from C to F, meanwhile, involves an interval called a fourth.

◇ If you already know the size of one interval, it's easy to compare it to other intervals around it, rather than counting the steps every time. The interval from C to A—moving from C to D, E, F, G, and A—produces a sixth.

◇ Moving from C to D, E, F, G, A, and finally to B on step seven produces a seventh. Moving eight steps is not called an eighth but rather an octave, but the concept is the same.

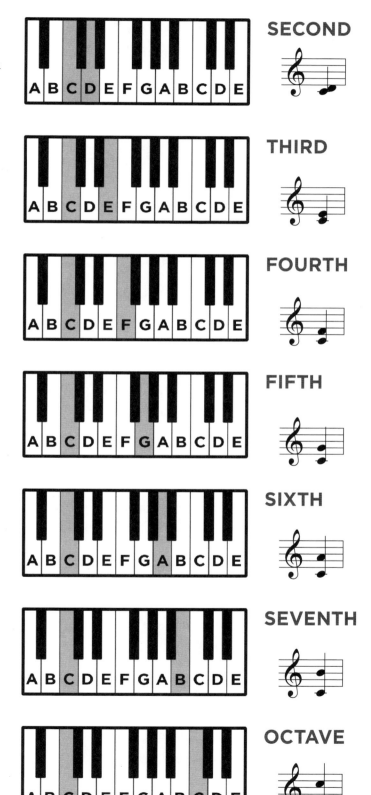

SECOND

THIRD

FOURTH

FIFTH

SIXTH

SEVENTH

OCTAVE

One of the mistakes students often make is forgetting to count the starting note. It is counterintuitive. In other circumstances, whether you're counting the number of moves in a board game or the number of stops on your commute, you never count where you started as step one. But in music, dealing with intervals presents something of a unique case: You always count the starting note as the first step.

Interval Quality

◇ Interval size is just one part of describing the distance between two notes. Another part to the equation is the quality of the interval. For instance, take the distance between C and D on the keyboard. This is a whole step, separated by the half step of the black key (which can be notated as a raised C-sharp or a lowered D-flat.) The whole step from C to D can be called a second.

◇ If a whole step is described as a second, what about a half step? In this case, the half step is the interval from C to D-flat. It's a smaller interval than the whole step, but it is also called a second. To describe the difference, the quality of the interval is helpful.

◇ There are five different qualities that an interval can present: major, minor, augmented, diminished, and perfect. To help you understand this, the C major scale is a useful example. All of the intervals in this scale—starting on C and then moving up to each new note—are either a major interval or a perfect interval.

❑ The interval from C to D is a major second.
❑ C to E is a major third.
❑ C to F is a perfect fourth.
❑ C to G is a perfect fifth.
❑ C to A is a major sixth.
❑ C to B is a major seventh.
❑ And C to C is a perfect octave.

◇ A relevant question here is this: Why are the fourth, fifth, and octave intervals perfect instead of major? They are never referred to as major or minor intervals. The reason can be traced all the way back to the beginnings of harmony in Western music.

◇ When single-melody chants in the Christian church first became harmonized by adding additional voices, the first interval used was the octave, followed closely by the fifth, as it was deemed to be a pleasing, open sonority similar to an octave.

◇ Both intervals sound open and resonate. The fourth was soon added, and it shares a similar open sound with the fifth. Ever since that time, all three of these intervals have been known as perfect.

- That covers two of the five qualities that an interval can present: major and perfect. To find the other three—minor, augmented, and diminished—it is necessary to adjust the major and perfect intervals.

    ❑ Making any major third a half step smaller will change the quality of the interval from major to minor. For instance, take the major third from C to E. Lowering the E to E-flat makes the major third a half step smaller.

    ❑ Next, regarding diminished intervals, consider the perfect fifth between C and G. When a perfect interval is made smaller by a half step, it becomes diminished. C to G-flat is a diminished fifth.

    ❑ Finally, to understand augmented intervals, consider the perfect fourth between C and F. Raising the F by a half step to F-sharp makes the interval bigger, and the result is called an augmented fourth.

MINOR THIRD

AUGMENTED FOURTH

DIMINISHED FIFTH

Interval Relations

- This lesson concludes with a look at how these intervals are related to one another. There are two broad categories of intervals: consonant and dissonant intervals.

- Dissonant intervals are so named because of the biting, jarring quality of their sound. Tritones, the seconds (both major and minor), and the sevenths (also both major and minor) are dissonant intervals. (For more on tritones, refer to the video lesson.)

- The consonant intervals, on the other hand, sound pleasant and harmonious. These include the perfect intervals of the fourth, fifth, and octave. Specifically, these are called perfect consonances.

- The remaining intervals—the thirds and the sixths, and both the major and minor versions of each—are also consonant. However, these are called imperfect consonances to distinguish them from the perfect intervals. Contrary to the dissonant intervals, consonant intervals feel much more stable and potentially are points of rest in a composition.

◇ Dissonant intervals aren't just unstable. They also have a strong pull to resolve to the consonant intervals. And this is one of the most important factors that drives Western tonal music. The continuous back and forth between consonance, dissonance, and consonance again is the foundation on which tonal music functions.

QUESTIONS TO CONSIDER

1 What are the two ways to describe the distance between two notes?

2 What is the difference between consonant and dissonant intervals?

EXERCISE: Intervals

Identify and label the following intervals.

Above each note, write in a note that will create the indicated interval.

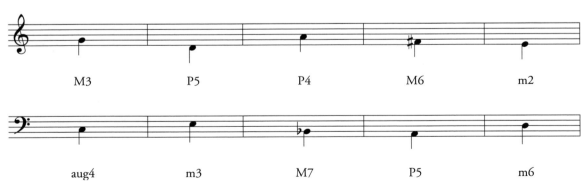

M3   P5   P4   M6   m2

aug4   m3   M7   P5   m6

Answers for Intervals Exercise

Identify and label the following intervals.

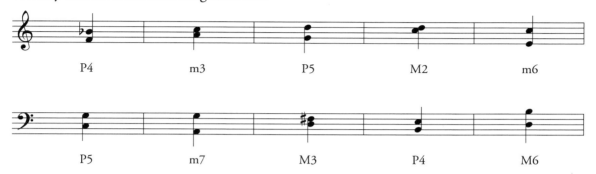

Above each note, write in a note that will create the indicated interval.

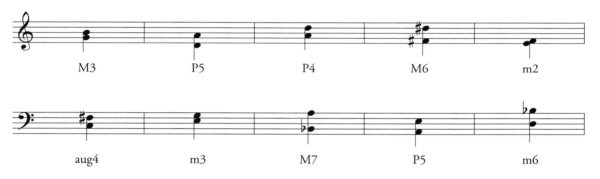

Blank staves for practicing intervals can be found at the back of the book.

The Circle of Fifths

This lesson discusses the highly organized nature of tonal music. Specifically, it looks at how music handles sharps and flats, and it focuses largely on key signatures. The lesson also introduces the circle of fifths.

Key Signatures

⬧ The key signature of a piece conveys two critical pieces of information. It tells you which notes will be sharp and flat. It also tells you which scale is going to be used throughout the piece. For example, a key signature bearing one sharp informs us that the music will primarily make use of the notes appearing in a G major scale.

⬧ The key signature is always found at the very beginning of the music, and—except for the key of C major—it will display sharps or flats. Because the C major scale doesn't include any sharps or flats, its key signature displays none of them. The absence of flats and sharps from the key signature is a good indicator that the music is probably in the key of C major.

⬧ The sharps and flats in a key signature are always presented in the same order. The first sharp will always be F-sharp, which indicates the key of G major. That is

followed by C-sharp, G-sharp, and D-sharp. The key signature for D major has two sharps, and the key signature for E major has four sharps.

⬧ Since there are seven notes in a scale, it's possible to have up to seven sharps in a key signature. Adding a fifth sharp, A-sharp, would create the key signature of B major. A sixth sharp, E-sharp, would create F-sharp major, and the last sharp, B-sharp, would create C-sharp major.

⬧ The order of flats in a key signature starts with B-flat, denoting the key of F major. The next flat is E-flat, indicating B-flat major. A-flat is the third flat, indicating E-flat major, followed by D-flat, which denotes A-flat major. The fifth flat is G-flat, creating D-flat major, followed by the sixth flat, C-flat, which creates G-flat major. The final flat, F-flat, creates the key of C-flat major.

C Major | G Major | D Major | A Major | E Major | B Major | F♯ Major | C♯ Major

F Major | B♭ Major | E♭ Major | A♭ Major | D♭ Major | G♭ Major | C♭ Major

---

AN ONLINE KEY SIGNATURE TOOL

The website MusicTheory.net has a helpful tool for working on key signatures:
https://www.musictheory.net/exercises/keysig/d999yydyyyyy

The Circle of Fifths

- The circle of fifths reveals one of the core features of tonal music: a highly organized system in which the keys are all related to each other. The keys are positioned by the interval of a fifth.

- The circle of fifths summarizes some of the key changes that commonly take place in music. Music often moves to new keys within a single piece. When that happens— when the key changes mid-piece—it is called a modulation.

- Clockwise motion around the circle adds sharps to the key signatures. And counterclockwise motion adds flats to the key signatures. The circle also provides a great reference tool as you learn the various key signatures.

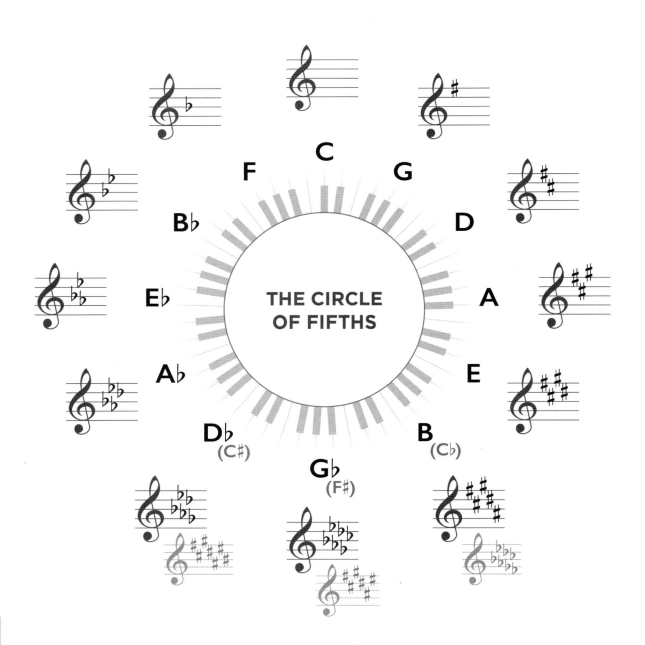

QUESTIONS TO CONSIDER

1 How are the different major scales in music related to each other?

2 What does the circle of fifths reveal about the way tonal music is organized?

EXERCISE: Major Key Signatures

Identify each major key from the key signatures.

Provide the correct major key signatures for the indicated keys.

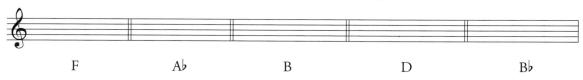

F   A♭   B   D   B♭

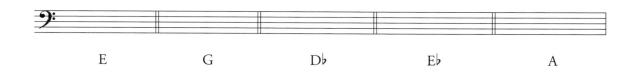

E   G   D♭   E♭   A

𝄢 Answers for Major Key Signatures Exercise

Identify each major key from the key signatures.

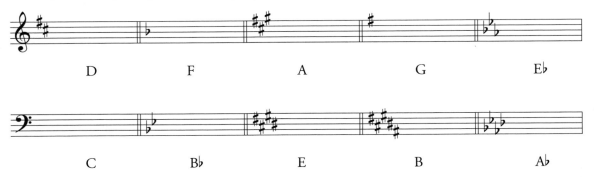

D   F   A   G   E♭

C   B♭   E   B   A♭

Provide the correct major key signatures for the indicated keys.

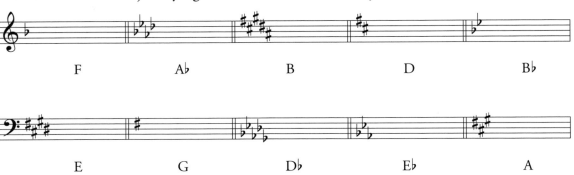

F   A♭   B   D   B♭

E   G   D♭   E♭   A

Meter: How Music Moves

Music is unique among the arts in the way it incorporates time. The notes on the page represent what the music will sound like. But knowing when to play the notes is just as important as the notes themselves. In music, a sense of time is essential both to how the art form is expressed and how it will be understood.

Meter and Measures

◇ Segmenting a piece of music into smaller, more manageable chunks makes it easier to read rhythms and follow along. Those smaller segments in a musical score are known as measures.

◇ A measure consists of a predetermined number of units, which are called beats. There are often two, three, or four beats, but other numbers are possible, too.

◇ The meter of a piece of music describes how many beats are in each measure. Saying that the meter of a piece is "in four," for instance, means that each measure will have four beats.

◇ The meter in music is advertised right at the beginning of the score with the meter signature. The $\frac{4}{4}$ meter signature indicates that there are four beats in each measure. This is one of the most common meters in music, especially in more popular music genres such as pop and rock. It's so common that musicians refer to it as common time.

◇ Specifically, the number on top of the meter signature tells the musician how many beats to expect in each measure. The number on the bottom tells what kind of note will be associated with the beat. In a $\frac{4}{4}$ meter, the 4 on the bottom indicates that a quarter note will get the beat. In other words, every count will be equivalent to a quarter note.

◇ A quarter note has a filled-in note head with a long stem. That stem will go up or down depending on where it is positioned on the staff.

◇ Eighth notes are exactly half the value of a quarter note. In other words, you need two of them to account for a full beat in $\frac{4}{4}$ time. Subdividing a quarter note, or single beat, doesn't change the meter. There are still four beats in the measure, but subdividing the beat allows for more complex rhythms.

◇ Quarter notes and eighth notes are only two note values out of a large family of possibilities. They can also be shorter or longer. For example, an eighth note can be divided into two smaller parts called sixteenth notes. A second flag on the stem of the sixteenth note visually distinguishes it from an eighth note. Two sixteenth notes are equal to one eighth note in time length. Smaller divisions are possible, too.

◇ It is also possible to go the other way. For instance, combining two quarter notes produces a half note. A half note looks like a quarter note, except the note head is hollow. In a $\frac{4}{4}$ measure, the half note takes up two beats—that is, half the measure.

◇ A whole note, meanwhile, accounts for four beats of a $\frac{4}{4}$ measure. Combining four quarter notes or two half notes results in a whole note. It looks like a half note without a stem.

Rests

- Resting places are essential in music. They introduce separation and distance between notes. Rests come with their own symbols but work along the same naming structure as notes do.

- A quarter rest will be the same length as a quarter note, but it signals silence. Eighth rests look like an ornate number 7. The top of the rest symbol resembles the flag on an eighth note.

- Adding another one makes it a sixteenth rest, and so on. A half rest looks somewhat like a top hat: a small rectangle that sit on the staff line. A whole rest is visually similar to the half rest, but it hangs below the staff line.

QUARTER   EIGHTH   SIXTEENTH   HALF   WHOLE

The term syncopation *refers to any rhythm pattern that emphasizes notes off the main beat. Offbeat rhythms occur everywhere in music but are very common in world music and jazz.*

Dots and Beams

- Another important concept of rhythm and note length is known as the dot, because that's how it's indicated. When a small dot is placed after a note, it adds to the length of that note by a half.

- For example, consider a quarter note. Placing a dot after the note head increases the length of the note by one half of the note's value. Half of a quarter note is an eighth note, so a dotted quarter note will last the length of a quarter note plus an eighth note.

- Dots can be applied to any note. The resulting length will always be the original note's time value plus half of its time value. A dotted half note, for instance, lasts the equivalent of three quarter notes.

- When groups of eighth notes are written together, sometimes the individual flags are replaced by long beams. This makes the passages somewhat easier to read because they are less cluttered on the page. If groups of sixteenth notes are needed, a second beam will be added, and so on.

Resources

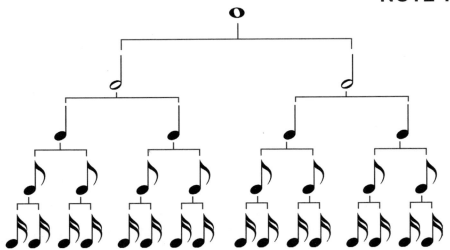

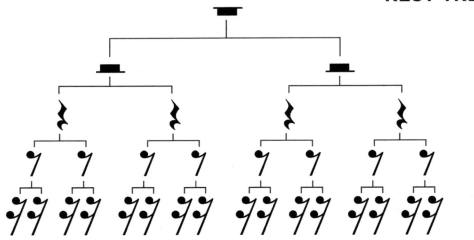

QUESTIONS TO CONSIDER

1 How do we account for the passage of time in a piece of music?

2 What do various different meters in music sound like?

Simple and Compound Meters

Most of the music people listen to is grouped into repeating units that are two, three, or four beats in length. However, the way those individual beats are subdivided can have a dramatic effect on the music. This lesson looks at simple meters and compound meters.

Two Equal Parts

- Some music subdivides each beat into two equal parts. Take John Philip Sousa's march "Hail to the Spirit of Liberty," which has a meter signature known as cut time. This is represented by the letter C with a line through the middle (¢). The symbol is a stand-in for the meter signature of $\frac{2}{2}$.

- The upper number of the meter signature indicates that there are two beats in every measure. The lower number, 2, tells us that the half note is the note value that gets the beat. In other words, you can expect to see two half-note beats in each measure.

- When the beat of a piece of music is subdivided into two equal parts, the meter is described as a simple meter. Marches, with only a few exceptions, are typically written in simple meters.

Three Equal Parts

- Some music subdivides each beat into three equal parts. When music has a beat that is subdivided into groups of three, the music is using a compound meter. For instance, the signature of $\frac{6}{8}$ is a big clue that the music will subdivide each beat into groups of three.

- Compound meters always feature a dotted note as the main beat in a measure. The time value of dotted notes is equal to the designated note's full value plus half again. For example, a dotted quarter note is equal to a quarter note plus an eighth note. Stated another way, a dotted quarter note can also be counted off as three eighth notes. Two dotted quarter notes are equal in value to six eighth notes.

- In $\frac{2}{4}$ time, there are two beats, and the quarter note gets the beat. Following the same logic, the $\frac{6}{8}$ meter signature would suggest that there are six beats in the measure and that the eighth note gets the beat. But this is not the case. Remember, this is a compound meter, not simple meter.

- There are six eighth notes in the measure. The meter signature is revealing something about the meter, but it's referring to the subdivision of the beats rather than to the main beats. Because there is no individual number to represent the time value of a dotted quarter note, meter is represented via subdivisions in compound meter.

- In general, any meter signature with a number 6 on top indicates a compound meter consisting of two main beats. If the compound meter has three main beats, that necessitates three sub-beats and a 9 for the top number. If there are four main beats, that would call for yet another three sub-beats and a 12 for the top number.

- You can think of it this way: $\frac{2}{4}$ and $\frac{6}{8}$ are very similar meters. They both have two main beats, but the only difference is the subdivision of the beat. The meter signatures are admittedly a confusing aspect of compound meter, but just remember that top numbers of 6, 9, and 12 almost always indicate compound meters.

Examples of Compound Meter

THE TAKADIMI SYSTEM

See the PDF in this link for information on the Takadimi system:
https://jmtp.appstate.edu/takadimi-beat-oriented-system-rhythm-pedagogy

QUESTIONS TO CONSIDER

1 What is the difference between simple and compound meters?

2 What are the difficulties in distinguishing meters while listening to music?

Downbeats and Upbeats: Performing Rhythm

Music is an active art form. It requires action on the part of the performer to be created as well as action from the listener to be understood. This lesson's video component shows how to clap out different rhythms that are more or less standard in different genres of music. This guidebook chapter summarizes and reviews certain information regarding those rhythms.

Simple Rhythms

◇ An example of a simple rhythm is four quarter notes in a single $\frac{4}{4}$ measure. The meter signature reveals that there are four beats in the measure, and the quarter note gets the beat.

◇ An eighth note gets exactly half the time value of a quarter note. Therefore, it takes two eighth notes to fill one beat in $\frac{4}{4}$.

◇ One of the best-known rhythms in popular music can be heard in the "stomp, stomp, clap" pattern from the beginning of the Queen song "We Will Rock You." It involves an alternative of eighth-note pairs and a single quarter note. Many other songs use this rhythm, including Shania Twain's "Any Man of Mine" and Eminem's "'Till I Collapse."

◇ Queen wanted this rhythm to be a simple, compelling invitation for the crowds at their shows to participate in making the music with them. It has proven simple and extremely effective.

Rhythm Concepts

◇ Remember that a dot next to a note adds exactly half of that note's time value. For example, a dotted quarter note at the beginning gets the same amount of time as a quarter note and an eighth note combined. You can also think of it as equal to the duration of three eighth notes.

◇ A dotted eighth note is equal to an eighth note plus a sixteenth note. It's common to see a sixteenth note paired with a dotted eighth note.

◇ You can hear dotted notes in action in Robert Schumann's Symphony no. 3. This piece of music features dotted notes at the beginning of the second movement.

◇ It also features something known as a pickup measure, which is scored by the single eighth note at the beginning. This pickup note isn't part of a full measure of music. Instead, it's simply an extra note before the movement begins. The figure below demonstrates the rhythm of the first four measures of Schumann's Symphony no. 3.

PICKUP MEASURE

◇ Ties are another common rhythmic instruction you will encounter. Ties are curved lines that connect notes together, combining their lengths. Like dots, they extend the length of a note.

◇ A dotted quarter note has exactly the same time value as a quarter note tied to an eighth note. However, ties are more flexible than dotted notes, because ties can connect any note to any adjacent note of any time value.

Although music meter tends to be structured rigidly on the page, a performance can be very fluid.

Compound and Swing Meters

◇ A compound meter differs from a simple meter in the subdivisions of the beat. Compound meters split each beat into three sub-beats instead of two. The figure at right shows an example of a compound meter.

Compound meter can be tricky, especially right after working with simple meters. If you need to, spend some time practicing by clapping along with the video lesson's examples.

◇ The rhythmic style known as swing is often found in jazz music. It's like a relaxed version of the aforementioned pattern that uses dotted eighth and sixteenth notes.

◇ However, in jazz, the rhythm isn't typically notated with dotted notes because it is a stylistic expectation. The sheet music sometimes includes the word *swing* to indicate that expectation. The amount of swing a note gets often varies between pieces and performers.

QUESTIONS TO CONSIDER

1 How are rhythms represented in written music?

2 What does it feel like to perform rhythms from a score?

Minor Keys

This lesson focuses on minor keys, which many people associate with tragic moments and sad emotions. It looks at the difference between major and minor keys and reintroduces the circle of fifths, which also appears in an earlier lesson and is a helpful tool for this one.

C Major and C Minor

- The C major scale consists of the notes C, D, E, F, G, A, B, and another C on top. It has no sharps or flats, and neither does the key signature for C major.

- The C major scale transforms into the C minor scale with three note changes. The first—and most important—note to change is the scale's third note: E. This note is referred to by its functional name (the mediant) or by its position, which is known as the scale degree.

- Since it is the third note in the scale, E is called scale-degree three. When this note is lowered by a half step from E to E-flat, the minor quality becomes apparent.

- The next note to change is the submediant: the sixth note, or scale-degree six. That would be A. Lowering it a half step creates A-flat.

- The final note to change is known as the leading tone. It is the seventh note, or scale-degree seven, which is B. Once again, it is lowered a half step to B-flat. With the three note changes, the C minor scale is complete, incorporating these notes: C, D, E-flat, F, G, A-flat, B-flat, C.

- That's all it takes to convert a major scale into a minor scale. To recap, the steps were to simply lower the mediant, the submediant, and the leading tone by a half step.

Ludwig van Beethoven composed the Coriolan Overture, which makes use of a minor key, in 1807 as the introduction to a theatrical play of the same name. The play follows the exploits of the 5th-century BCE Roman general Coriolanus. Late in his life, Coriolanus defects from his own army and leads enemy forces against Rome. His mother and wife plead with him to cease the attack, and he eventually withdraws his forces. Unable to ever return home, he ends his own life in the story's tragic conclusion. Beethoven's use of a minor key for this overture seems to make sense, given the tragic nature of the story.

Parallel Scales and Key Signatures

⟡ The scales C major and C minor are referred to as parallel scales. Parallel scales are major and minor scales that share the same starting note. This relationship highlights the similar starting notes, but it also distinguishes them as different types of scales.

⟡ You can use the three lowered notes to determine a key signature for the C minor scale. The three flats of B-flat, E-flat, and A-flat represent the key of C minor. These same three flats also make up the key signature for E-flat major. In other words, E-flat major and C minor share the same key signature.

⟡ Every key signature for the major keys also corresponds with a minor key. And major and minor keys that share the same key signature form pairs of relative scales. In this relationship, the keys share the same key signature but not the same starting note.

⟡ The circle of fifths, introduced in lesson 5, is an organizational tool that shows all of the possible major keys and how they are related. Moving clockwise around the circle, each new key is described by the addition of a sharp to the key signature. Below is the circle of fifths again for reference.

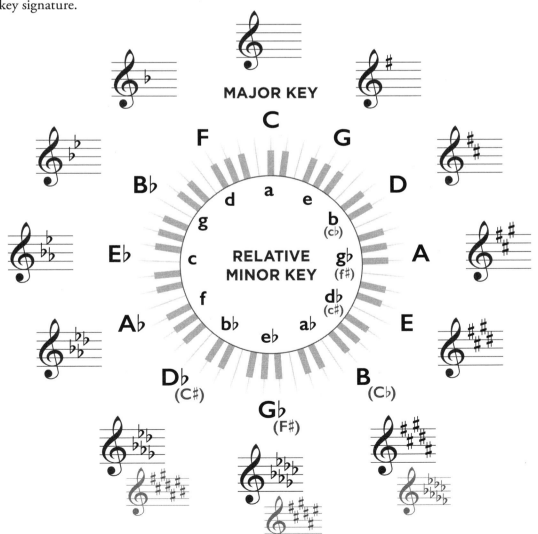

Flavors of Minor Scales

When minor keys are used in music, composers often make subtle changes to the scale, depending on the context of the music. These flavors add subtle but important distinctions.

The first of these three flavors is the natural minor. It's the naturally occurring form of the scale, with no changes or alterations. But this flavor of the scale is actually the least commonly used.

The second—and by far the most commonly used—flavor is harmonic minor. This takes the natural minor scale and raises scale-degree seven. That restores the note to the way it exists in the major scale.

Meanwhile, melodic minor raises scale-degrees six and seven, but only in melodic passages when the music moves up.

QUESTIONS TO CONSIDER

1 How are major and minor keys related?

2 Do minor keys always represent sadness in music?

 ## EXERCISE: Minor Key Signatures

Identify each minor key from the key signatures.

Provide the correct minor key signatures for the indicated keys.

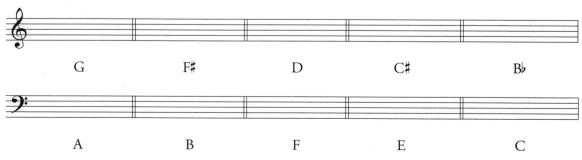

♮: Answers for Minor Key Signatures Exercise

Identify each minor key from the key signatures.

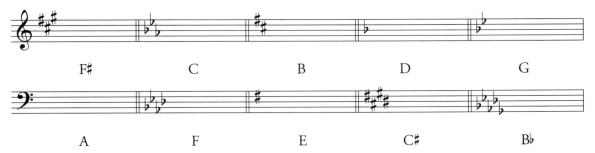

F♯   C   B   D   G

A   F   E   C♯   B♭

Provide the correct minor key signatures for the indicated keys.

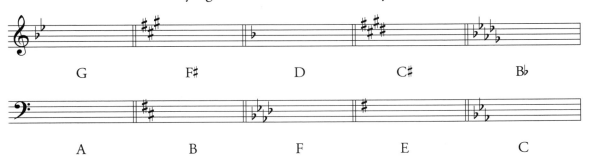

G   F♯   D   C♯   B♭

A   B   F   E   C

LESSON 10

Dynamics, Articulation, and Tempo

This lesson engages with dynamics—that is, how loud or soft music is played. It also introduces the concepts of articulation—how each note is performed—and tempo—how fast or slow the music moves. Musical markings in the score reflecting each of these help the music come alive in performance.

Dynamics

◇ Dynamic markings in a score can be shown in a few different ways. The most common is through the use of the markings *f*, *m*, and *p*. These are abbreviations for the Italian words *forte*, *mezzo*, and *piano*. In a musical context, the term *forte* calls for musicians to play loudly, and *piano* calls for them to play softly.

◇ The term *mezzo*, meaning "half," is always paired with other dynamic marks. When paired with the *piano* mark, it indicates soft playing, but not as soft as *piano* alone. When *mezzo* is paired with *forte*, it indicates loud playing, but not as loud as *forte*.

◇ Dynamics do not have to change suddenly. For example, a decrescendo is a graphical indication for the player to reduce the volume of the notes over the length of the symbol's lines. A crescendo, meanwhile, calls for an increase in volume. Composers will sometimes use the written abbreviations *cresc.* or *decresc.* to indicate these gradual changes.

crescendo

decrescendo

Articulation

◇ Next, this lesson turns to articulation. In music, the term *articulation* refers to how a note or a group of notes is played. They can be played as extremely sharp, short notes; as long, smooth, connected notes; or something in between. In music, several symbols convey the different ways that notes can be articulated.

◇ A curved line is an articulation marking called a slur. It indicates to the performer to play the notes with as little space between them as possible. This results in melodic lines that are smooth and connected.

◇ Small dots above or below notes are staccato marks, and they are essentially the opposite of a slur. Staccato markings direct the performer to play the notes with an abundance of space between the notes.

◇ Tenuto markings, which resemble lines above or below notes, tell the musician to make the notes indicated slightly longer than their normal value. These notes are also slurred.

◇ Accent marks tell the performer to play the note a little more forcefully than the notes around it. This is typically accomplished by playing the note slightly louder than the others.

◇ A wavy line above or below a note is called a mordent. A mordent instructs the performer to play a little turn on that note, embellishing it.

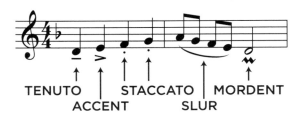

TENUTO ACCENT STACCATO SLUR MORDENT

Tempo

◇ This lesson concludes with a look at tempo—the speed at which music is played. Unlike dynamics, tempos tend to be more objective, thanks in large part to the metronome. A metronome is a music device that produces a steady pulse at different speeds. The first modern metronomes were produced around the beginning of the 19th century.

◇ Metronome speeds are measured as beats per minute, or BPM. A tempo of 60 BPM is fairly slow: one per second. You might see this music described with the Italian words *lento* or *largo*. Both words mean "slow."

◇ Doubling the tempo to 120 beats a minute creates a much brisker pace. This tempo is often described with the term *allegro*, which is translated from Italian as "cheerful." Even faster tempos—around 160 BPM—are often described by the word *vivace*, translated as "lively" or "very fast."

◇ The abbreviation *rit.* stands for the term *ritardando*. This is an indication for the players to slow down gradually over the span of music as indicated by the dashes after the abbreviation. How much the music slows is usually an interpretative decision made by the performers. Later, the words *a tempo* might appear. This is an indication to resume the original tempo.

◇ An important consideration of tempo in musical performance is the concept of rubato. Rubato is sometimes a specific performance indication. But more generally, it's the concept that music should not be performed rigidly, in a single tempo. Instead, music often ebbs and flows through a number of different tempi.

◇ Performers expressively slow down and speed up as they play, offering their own interpretation of the music. Composers have ways to change the tempo during a piece, too.

QUESTIONS TO CONSIDER

1 How do we describe the speed at which music is performed?

2 What are the different ways that written music indicates how loud or soft it should be played?

Counterpoint: Composing with Two Voices

Mozart composed the simple tune "Ah, vous dirai-je, Maman" in 1781. The melody originated in France during the middle of the 18th century, and Mozart developed his theme and variations off of it. Today, you might hear it as "Twinkle, Twinkle, Little Star." On the keyboard, the "Twinkle, Twinkle, Little Star" melody is played by the right hand. The left hand provides harmonic support. The music for the right and left hands is made up of single melodic lines. When two melodic lines are written to be played at the same time, that is called counterpoint.

The video component of this lesson shows how to compose a two-line counterpoint melody. This guidebook chapter summarizes certain key ideas from the lesson.

Background on Counterpoint

The art of counterpoint has been around since the beginning of Western art music, which is typically thought of as music composed in the Western world starting around 1600. But the rules of composing with counterpoint have evolved over the centuries, as musical styles changed. Most music composed in a classical Western style is based on counterpoint, in some way.

The 18th-century composer and music theorist Johann Fux wrote the first comprehensive treatise on counterpoint and how to teach it. Titled *Gradus ad Parnassum*, or *The Steps to Parnassus*, it is written as a dialogue between a master teacher and a motivated though naive student. Their conversations, and printed examples, guide readers through the rules of counterpoint.

Theme from
"Ah, vous dirai-je, Maman"

Mozart

Types of Motion

- In his aforementioned tune, Mozart uses motion between the two melodic parts. Motion refers to how the parts move in relation to each other. Note that the different melodic parts of counterpoint are often called voices, even though no one actually sings in this example.

- There are four basic motion types in music. The first is called oblique motion. It occurs when one voice remains on the same note while the other voice moves. This motion type is at the very beginning of "Twinkle, Twinkle." On a piano, as the right hand stays on the note C, the left hand moves from a low C to a high C.

- The "Twinkle, Twinkle" melody repeats almost every note throughout. Oblique motion caused by those repeating notes is quite common in this musical example, occurring in practically every measure.

- The next motion type is called similar motion. It occurs when the voices move in the same direction—up or down—but not by the same interval. For instance, from the second beat of measure 1 to the first beat of measure 2, the right hand moves up by a

perfect fifth from C to G. The left hand also moves up, but it does so by a major third from C to E.

- The third motion type is contrary motion. This occurs when the voices move in opposite directions. In this motion type, the size of the intervals doesn't matter so long as one is moving up and the other is moving down. This occurs in the Mozart theme when moving from the second beat of measure 3 to the first beat of measure 4.

- The fourth and final motion type is parallel motion. This is like similar motion, when the voices move in the same direction. But in parallel motion, the voices also move by the same interval size.

- In the Mozart theme, this occurs only three times, in measures 15 and 16. The right hand moves up from E to F. That interval is a second. And the left hand moves at the same time from C to D, which is also a second. Though the tonal quality of the intervals is different, all moves of the same size are classified as parallel. These notes then fall back to C and E, then move down by a second again to B and D, all in parallel motion.

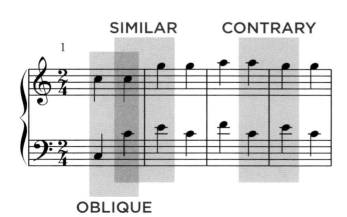

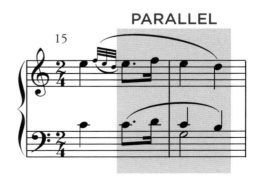

Interval Sizes

◇ Next, this lesson turns to look at the interval size between two lines of counterpoint. In the type of counterpoint covered in this lesson, some intervals are just about always OK to use. Some are OK some of the time. And some are better avoided.

◇ You can use major or minor thirds and major or minor sixths at any point in your counterpoint. These are all consonant intervals. Consonant intervals sound pleasant and harmonious. As such, they can come and go during a piece without needing any special care.

◇ Perfect octaves and perfect fifths are also consonant. But they must adhere to one constraint in counterpoint: These perfect intervals cannot be written in parallel motion. In other words, a perfect octave cannot move to another perfect octave in parallel motion. The motion of parallel perfect intervals is considered to be too open, creating a hollow sound that is undesirable.

◇ Some intervals aren't used at all between the voices in this lesson's style of counterpoint. Major and minor seconds and major sevenths aren't used. The dissonances are just too biting.

◇ Another interval that is not allowed between the voices is the perfect fourth. This might seem strange, given that the interval is consonant. But the restriction goes back to the early era of Western music. From early on, a perfect fourth was considered a dissonant interval when created with the lowest-sounding voice.

◇ Finally, as for special intervals, diminished fifths, augmented fourths, and minor sevenths are allowed only if the next interval properly resolves the dissonance.

QUESTIONS TO CONSIDER

1 What is counterpoint, and what does it reveal about the structure of tonal music?

2 What are the rules to composing music using counterpoint?

EXERCISE: Counterpoints

Create a melody above each given melody following the rules of counterpoint. There are multiple copies of the score so that you can try this exercise more than once.

Musical Harmony: Triads

This lesson dives into the concept of harmony—that is, when two or more notes sound simultaneously. The lesson investigates how harmonies are created and describes how they interact. An understanding of harmony is vital to a full understanding of the fundamentals of music. The video lesson delves into specific pieces of music; this guidebook chapter covers some important terms and concepts related to triads.

Major and Minor Triads

◇ Chords are any combination of three or more notes heard at the same time. In Western tonal music, various combinations of major and minor third intervals create most of the chords we hear.

◇ As a rule, any group of three notes—each separated by a third—is called a triad. A minor third is an interval that encompasses three half steps, or semitones.

◇ When the first third is a major third, and the third above that is a minor third, it is called a major triad. An example is the D major triad, which uses D, F-sharp, and A. The interval from D to F-sharp is a major third, and the interval from F-sharp to A is a minor third.

◇ The lowest note in this group of thirds is the note on which the harmony is based. It is called the root of the chord. In this case, it is D.

◇ The major triads are associated with happy, positive emotions. Minor triads are associated with sadder ones. Major and minor triads are by far the most common triads in Western music.

◇ Triad inversion occurs when the lowest-sounding note of a chord is something other than the root. In a first inversion triad, for instance, the third of the harmony is the lowest note.

◇ First inversion triads are quite common in Western tonal music, and they have a similar overall sound as a root-position triad. The difference is subtle, yet it adds a tiny bit of variety in any progression of harmonies.

D MAJOR TRIAD

ROOT POSITION   FIRST INVERSION

Diminished and Augmented Triads

◇ Though major and minor triads are the most common triads in tonal music, there are also two other types of triads that can be used. Diminished triads are one. They use stacked minor thirds, with an example combination being A-sharp, C-sharp, and E. These notes create a minor third from A-sharp to C-sharp and another minor third from C-sharp to E.

DIMINISHED

◇ Diminished triads are used less frequently than major or minor triads. But the sound they create is biting and dissonant, offering a nice contrast. Diminished harmonies also create a bit of tension in the progression that eventually must be released, helping to propel the music forward.

◇ A final type of triad in tonal music is an augmented triad. Augmented triads are uncommon in most tonal music. The best way to illustrate one is to start first with a major triad. For instance, starting with a D major triad, raising the fifth up by a half step from A to A-sharp creates an augmented triad.

The augmented triad gets its name from the fifth. The fifth interval from D to A-sharp is an augmented fifth. The interval from D to F-sharp is a major third. And the interval from the F-sharp to A-sharp is also a major third. Two stacked major thirds will result in an augmented triad.

AUGMENTED

The following chart acts as a summary of the four types of triads that you will encounter in tonal music.

MAJOR (M)	major third + minor third (perfect fifth)
MINOR (m)	minor third + major third (perfect fifth)
DIMINISHED (°)	minor third + minor third (diminished fifth)
AUGMENTED (+)	major third + major third (augmented fifth)

QUESTIONS TO CONSIDER

1 What are the basic building blocks of harmony in tonal music?

2 How are harmonies analyzed in music, and how are they labeled on the score?

EXERCISE: Triads

Identify the root and quality of each triad.

Create each triad on the staff.

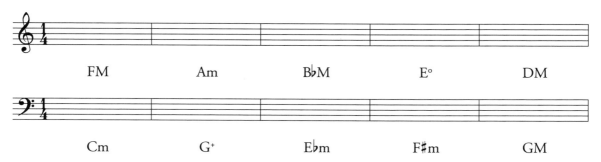

Answers for Triads Exercise

Identify the root and quality of each triad.

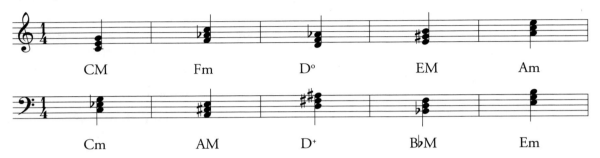

CM   Fm   D°   EM   Am

Cm   AM   D⁺   B♭M   Em

Create each triad on the staff.

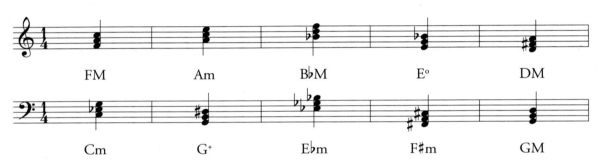

FM   Am   B♭M   E°   DM

Cm   G⁺   E♭m   F♯m   GM

LESSON 12—MUSICAL HARMONY: TRIADS

Musical Harmony: Seventh Chords

I f triads—groups of three notes separated by the interval of a third—are the basic building blocks of tonal music, then seventh chords are like colorful additions to the music. This lesson introduces seventh chords and shows how they are related to triads.

Basics on Seventh Chords

◇ A seventh chord is essentially a triad with one extra note. Take, for example, a D major triad. The notes of a triad are all separated by a third.

◇ Adding one more third on top of the triad creates a harmony with four notes, each separated from the other by a third. This is called a seventh chord because the interval from the root of the chord to the new note is a seventh.

◇ Seventh chords always have four notes. And just like triads, the notes of seventh chords can be stacked into third intervals. The names of the members of the seventh chord remain the same too. For example, in a chord from the Bach chorale discussed in the video lesson, the D on the bottom of the stack is the root, the F-sharp is the third, the A is the fifth, and the C is the seventh interval above the root. For this specific seventh chord based on D, it is a minor seventh from D up to C.

Just like triads, seventh chords can be inverted. That means that any member of the chord can be the lowest-sounding note.

◇ The first three notes of the stack—D, F-sharp, and A—form a triad. The first three notes of a seventh chord will always be a major, minor, or diminished triad.

◇ A major triad with an added minor third on top is sometimes called a major/minor seventh chord, but it is more frequently referred to as a dominant seventh chord. This is, by far, the most common seventh chord used in tonal music.

◇ Because of the frequency with which dominant seventh chords are used, you can simply add a superscripted 7 next to the root of the chord to indicate one. The D dominant seventh chord would simply be called D^7.

◇ A major seventh chord involves a major triad. For instance, in the case of a D major seventh chord, the triad would be D, F-sharp, and A. Then, it has a major third above the fifth. In this case, that would be C-sharp. To label this major seventh chord, you would write D, an uppercase M for "major," and then a superscripted 7: DM^7.

◇ There is a common type of seventh chord that contains a minor triad, and appropriately, it is called a minor seventh chord. It contains a minor triad—for example, D, F, and A—followed by another minor third, which is C in this case. The D minor seventh chord is notated in this manner: Dm^7.

SEVENTH CHORDS

DOMINANT (D⁷) MAJOR (DM⁷) MINOR (Dm⁷) *MINOR MAJOR (Dm^M⁷) DIMINISHED (D°⁷) HALF-DIMINISHED (Dø⁷)

There are two types of seventh chords that are based on diminished triads. Recall that a diminished triad is a stack of two minor thirds. If the root of the chord were a D, it would contain D, F, and A-flat. Each note is separated from the other by a minor third. Adding a minor third to the top of that D diminished triad incorporates a C-flat. This harmony is called a diminished seventh chord.

The second type of seventh chord that contains a diminished triad is called a half-diminished seventh chord. Instead of an additional minor third, it has a major third added.

The following chart acts as a summary of the seventh chords that you will encounter in tonal music.

DOMINANT (⁷)	major triad + minor third (minor seventh)
MAJOR (M⁷)	major triad + major third (major seventh)
MINOR (m⁷)	minor triad + minor third (minor seventh)
***MINOR MAJOR** (m^M⁷)	minor triad + major third (major seventh)
DIMINISHED (°⁷)	diminished triad + minor third (diminished seventh)
HALF-DIMINISHED (ø⁷)	diminished triad + major third (minor seventh)

QUESTIONS TO CONSIDER

1 What are seventh chords, and how are they different from triads?

2 Why is the fully diminished seventh chord unique?

---

* The minor major seventh chord is exceedingly rare in common-practice, Western tonal music.

EXERCISE: Seventh Chords

Identify the root and quality of each chord.

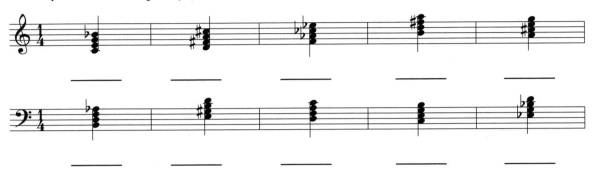

Create each chord on the staff.

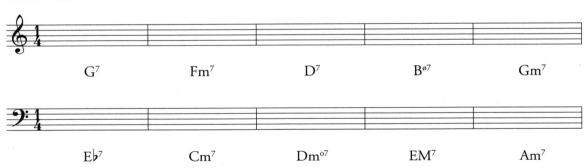

G⁷   Fm⁷   D⁷   B°⁷   Gm⁷

E♭⁷   Cm⁷   Dm°⁷   EM⁷   Am⁷

Answers for Seventh Chords Exercise

Identify the root and quality of each chord.

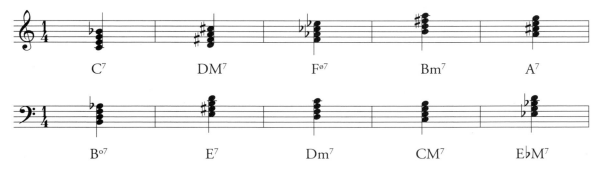

| C⁷ | DM⁷ | Fᵒ⁷ | Bm⁷ | A⁷ |

| Bᵒ⁷ | E⁷ | Dm⁷ | CM⁷ | E♭M⁷ |

Create each chord on the staff.

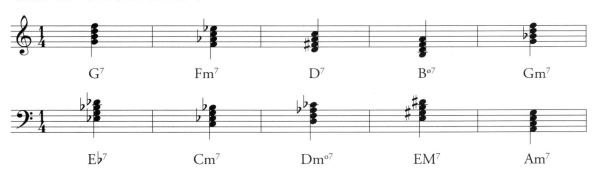

| G⁷ | Fm⁷ | D⁷ | Bᵒ⁷ | Gm⁷ |

| E♭⁷ | Cm⁷ | Dmᵒ⁷ | EM⁷ | Am⁷ |

Musical Harmony in Context: Progressions

Triads and seventh chords are the building blocks of harmony in Western tonal music. Based on stacks of intervals—stacks of thirds—these harmonies underlie much of the thinking behind how tonal music is written. But understanding the types and qualities of these chords is only a first step. To get a better picture of harmony in tonal music, one must also learn about harmonic function—that is, how the harmonies move from one to another within a given key. This lesson discusses three basic functions of tonal music.

Schumann's Symphony no. 3

◇ To understand this topic, a helpful example is the second movement of Robert Schumann's Symphony no. 3. A piano reduction of the first eight measures is shown below.

◇ The music is in the key of C major, and the first harmony of the piece sounds all throughout the entire first measure. The lowest note is a C. Most of the other notes are Es and Gs. When the notes are stacked in intervals of thirds, the result is a C major triad. Since the piece is in C major, you can call any C major triad you see by its other name: tonic. The tonic harmony is the home base for a piece of music. Just like the tonic note in a scale, the tonic harmony is usually where a piece will start. It's also where the piece will end.

◇ In the second measure, the first two beats again sound all of the notes of the C major—or tonic—triad. But on the third beat, the harmony changes. The lowest-sounding note is now a G. And the notes above it are G, B, and D. This is a G major triad.

◇ G is also the fifth note of the C major scale. That note is called the dominant. Subsequently, this triad—built on the fifth note of the scale—is the dominant harmony. The dominant acts as a foil to tonic. The dominant is the penultimate goal in a progression that eventually returns to the tonic. In the very next beat, the music does return to the tonic harmony: a C major triad.

◇ This is the way that almost all tonal music operates: cycling back and forth between the tonic and dominant harmonies, in a grand journey. Tonic and dominant are the two primary harmonic functions of tonal music.

Symphony no. 3
Measures 1–8, Piano Reduction

Robert Schumann

"An Wasserflüssen Babylon"

◇ The Johann Sebastian Bach chorale "An Wasserflüssen Babylon" has moments when tonic harmonies move to dominant and then back to tonic. This piece also introduces a new harmonic function. A piano reduction of the first two measures is shown below.

◇ This piece is in the key of G major, so any G major triads will be tonic triads. Additionally, any G major triad will have a tonic harmonic function.

◇ Recall that the dominant triad is based on the fifth note of the scale. In the key of G, that note is D. And building a triad based on D results in the notes D, F-sharp, and A. This creates a D major triad. Any D major triads will have a dominant function.

◇ The first harmony of the Bach chorale is a G major triad with G as the lowest-sounding note. It serves a tonic harmonic function.

◇ The next harmony is a C major triad with C as the lowest-sounding note. This triad serves as a harmonic function that fits between tonic and dominant. It is called a pre-dominant function.

◇ A pre-dominant harmony is often inserted between the tonic and dominant. This helps to create interest in the progression and prepares for the arrival of the dominant on its way back to the tonic.

◇ The terms *tonic*, *pre-dominant*, and *dominant* weren't around when Bach was writing music in the 18th century. However, the entire notion of harmonic function was largely based on a study of his chorales.

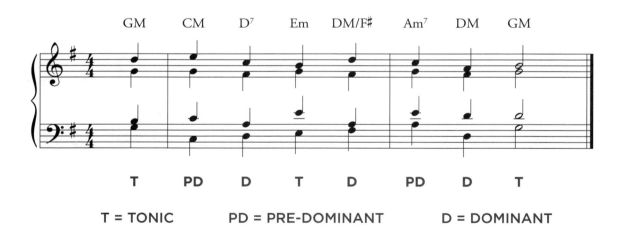

T = TONIC   PD = PRE-DOMINANT   D = DOMINANT

QUESTIONS TO CONSIDER

1 What are the three primary harmonic functions of tonal music?

2 How do the various harmonic functions interact in a progression of harmonies in music?

Musical Phrases and Cadences

Music is often written in many different sections, and even within a single movement, there can be even smaller sections. This lesson discusses the phrase structure of tonal music, specifically focusing on some of the most common kinds of harmonic cadences seen in Western classical music.

General Terms

Joseph Haydn's Symphony no. 45 is written in four large movements. The third movement is divided into yet smaller segments known as a minuet and a trio. This particular minuet was never meant to be danced to. However, it has many features of a minuet, including a time signature of $\frac{3}{4}$ and a strong emphasis on the first beat of each measure.

Even within these smaller sections of movements—even within a minuet, for instance—there can be still-smaller units of musical time. Musical phrases are one of the more useful delineations of these. Phrases are segments of music that end with some sense of rest or pause. That pause is often accompanied by a specific harmonic event called a cadence.

Cadences are harmonic progressions that help to signal some kind of ending. Whether it feels like a complete stop or a slight pause depends on the harmonies being used. Phrases almost always end with a musical cadence.

In symphonic compositions from the classical period of music, the third movement is often composed in the format of a minuet and trio. It's a tradition that incorporates older dance styles into concert music.

Half Cadences

In general, music theory recognizes two main kinds of cadences: half cadences and authentic cadences. The Clarinet Sonata written by Johannes Brahms is useful for examining half cadences. The first 12 measures of this piece are shown below.

The Brahms piece is written in the key of F minor, and it begins with a piano introduction followed by the entrance of the clarinet. The introduction continues until measure 12, at which point several things signal that this is the end of a phrase. The clarinet part rests, and the piano plays sustained notes.

The rest—a physical as well as musical expression—is the first element that helps identify a cadence and the end of a musical phrase. The second part of a phrase ending is the harmonic cadence. In this case, the harmony in measure 12 is a C major triad. A C major triad—built from the fifth note of the sonata's F minor scale—is the dominant triad. More importantly, this triad functions as the dominant harmony.

Any time a musical phrase ends with a dominant harmony, it is using a half cadence. A half cadence is named as such because it is a particularly weak cadence. It is a small interruption. This makes sense because the dominant function in music harmony always strives to ultimately return to the tonic function in a progression. Stopping on the dominant feels unsettled.

Clarinet Sonata
Measures 1–12

Johannes Brahms

Authentic Cadences

The counterpart to the half cadence—and the much stronger harmonic event—is the so-called authentic cadence. A piece with a good example of an authentic cadence is Johann Sebastian Bach's Goldberg Variations. The first eight measures of this piece are shown below.

The piece has a half cadence in measure 4. It reaches another pause at measure 8. On the second beat, the right and left hand both stop on half notes. The only other time this occurs is on the half cadence in measure 4.

This moment feels more complete than the half cadence in measure 4. It is a more definitive point of rest. The harmonic motion contributes to the finality of the moment.

There are a number of notes in this measure. The left-hand G is the lowest-sounding note. The right hand plays a B. The left hand also sounds a D at the end of the measure, spelling the complete G major triad.

A G major triad is tonic in the key of G major, and it therefore performs the tonic function. This cadence is preceded immediately by a dominant harmony.

There is a D dominant seventh chord in measure 7. D is the lowest-sounding note, with an F-sharp, A, and C above it. The other notes are melodic embellishments. This dominant harmony then moves directly to the G major tonic harmony in the next measure.

Goldberg Variations
Aria
Measures 1–8

Johann Sebastian Bach

Periods and Sentences

⋄ A weaker half cadence followed by a stronger authentic cadence, as shown in the Goldberg Variations example, is a common structure of two phrases in tonal music. The structure is known as a period. Periods are defined as two phrases in which the final cadence is stronger than the first cadence. Most of the time, that means a half cadence followed by an authentic cadence.

⋄ Periods are quite common in tonal music, especially in music composed during the classical era, which began around 1750 and ended around 1820. The classical era in music valued things such as symmetry and balance in music. Period structures are a great exemplar of that aesthetic.

⋄ In addition to being a period, the aforementioned eight measures of the Goldberg Variations are also a great example of another common feature in classical-era music called a sentence.

⋄ Measures 1 and 2 form a small two-measure unit all by themselves. There is no cadence, but a sense of pause in the music is there. Then, measures 3 and 4—leading up to the half cadence—form a group.

⋄ The music in measure 6 pushes ahead with a leap up to F-sharp, and it continues into measure 7. The music is now forming a longer four-measure group. In sum, the eight measures feature a two-measure group, a second two-measure group, and the four-measure group. This arrangement of groups is a common feature in tonal music known as a sentence. The pattern of two short ideas followed by a longer one is a universal concept in the world of tonal music.

QUESTIONS TO CONSIDER

1 What are half cadences and authentic cadences?

2 How do cadences and musical phrases work together to create larger structures in music?

LESSON 16

Hypermeter and Larger Musical Structures

The meter signature reveals how many beats are in a measure and what kind of note will get the beat. A meter signature of $\frac{4}{4}$ tells you to expect four beats in each measure, and the bottom 4 indicates that each beat is equivalent to a quarter note. In compound meter, however, the numbers in the meter signature describe subdivisions of the beat. The meter signature $\frac{6}{8}$ is one example of compound meter.

Simple and compound meter signatures both do a great job at conveying what to expect in each measure. But music is often grouped into larger structures. This lesson presents the idea that in addition to a meter signature, there's also a signature that tells you how many measures are in each phrase. This is called the hypermeter signature.

Haydn's Symphony no. 45

◇ To sample hypermeter, this lesson focuses on the beginning of the first movement of Joseph Haydn's Symphony no. 45. The first 34 measures of this piece are reproduced on the following pages.

◇ The meter signature is $\frac{3}{4}$, indicating that there are three quarter-note beats in each bar. This is simple meter since each main beat in the measure subdivides into two smaller sub-beats. The tempo marking *Allegro assai* translates to "very fast," meaning the music will move quickly.

◇ It moves so quickly that something interesting occurs for the listener. Some people hear groups of three quarter notes in each individual measure. Others hear the hypermeter—the motion from measure to measure.

◇ The Haydn piece provides a great example of the power of hypermeters. It is something like a Rorschach test for listening. Different people will experience the music in different ways.

Music Cognition and Hypermeter

◇ Music cognition is the study of how people perceive and understand the music they hear. Regarding tempo—or how fast or slow a piece of music moves—listeners tend to lock onto pulses comparable to the listener's heart rate. One study found that listeners lock onto a pulse somewhere in the range of 82 to 140 beats per minute, whether it be the beat of the written music or the hypermeter.

◇ In the video lesson, the TCU Symphony Orchestra performs the Haydn symphony at about 180 quarter-note beats per minute.

That's much brisker than the normal preference for hearing a pulse in music. On the other hand, the hypermeter pulse of this music—the rate at which each new measure begins—is about 60 beats per minute, which is below the preference established by the study.

◇ It makes sense, then, that some listeners gravitate to the faster pulse, while others are pulled to hear the slower pulse. The specific tempo of the piece doesn't give a clear direction toward either interpretation.

QUESTIONS TO CONSIDER

1 What is hypermeter, and how does it relate to regular meter?

2 How can finding the hypermeter in music help us understand the music better?

Symphony no. 45

Measures 1–34

Joseph Haydn

Understanding Music Lead Sheets

Lots of music is fully notated with notes, clefs, spelled-out harmonies, and numerous markings indicating dynamics, tempo, and articulations. But for the advanced musician—and the performing professional—music is often notated in a much more basic way: as a lead sheet. A lead sheet is a streamlined visual cue that typically consists of a single melody line. The harmonies are only suggested via a chord symbol above the notes. There are no indications of how loud or soft to play, no directions on how to play each note, and no specified instruments. This lesson explores lead sheet notation and discusses how to interpret what you're seeing on the page.

Lead Sheet: "Sweet Georgia Brown"

◇ The lead sheet for the original tune "Sweet Georgia Brown," written in 1925 by Ben Bernie and Maceo Pinkard, is shown on the following page.

◇ Most lead sheets are written using a treble clef. The melody tends to be played by higher-pitched instruments, so treble clef is generally better suited for scoring a lead sheet. Lead sheets, like traditional sheet music, also employ key signatures. "Sweet Georgia Brown" is likely to be in the key of F major, as indicated by the single flat in the key signature.

◇ All standard notational and meter rules apply. "Sweet Georgia Brown" is written in $\frac{4}{4}$, with four quarter-note beats per measure.

◇ The chord symbols themselves can vary depending on the music publisher. The first harmony in "Sweet Georgia Brown" is written as D^7. The letter always refers to the root of the chord: the note that the chord is built from.

◇ The number 7 indicates that this is a seventh chord, and specifically a dominant seventh chord. A dominant seventh chord contains a D major triad plus a minor third. After the first D^7, there isn't another chord symbol until measure 5. This means that the D^7 harmony should be played continuously over the first four measures.

◇ The next chord symbol, G^7, indicates a G dominant seventh chord. This moves to a C dominant seventh in measure 9 before arriving on an F major triad in measure 13. A single letter by itself in a lead sheet always indicates a major triad. Measure 16 displays a new chord symbol: Emi^7. This stands for an E minor seventh chord.

SWEET GEORGIA BROWN

BEN BERNIE
AND MACEO PINKARD

Lead Sheet: "Tea for Two"

◇ Next, this lesson turns to the lead sheet for "Tea for Two," written by Vincent Youmans. It features many more chord symbols, with chord changes roughly twice every measure. The four flats in the key signature indicate the song is in A-flat major.

◇ The tune starts by alternating back and forth between the B-flat minor seventh chord and an E-flat dominant seventh. In measure 3, there is an A-flat major seventh chord.

◇ As this piece is written in the key of A-flat major, the A-flat major seventh chord acts as the tonic. Jazz and popular tunes often use major seventh chords as the tonic.

◇ In measure 4, the symbol Bdim^7 indicates a B diminished seventh chord. A diminished seventh chord contains a diminished triad plus a minor third. You can also think of diminished seventh chords as a stack of minor thirds above the root. In this case, it calls for the notes B, D, F, and A-flat.

◇ Matters proceed without any new harmonies until measure 23. Then, there is a chord labeled as Cmi$^{7(\flat 5)}$. This label may look unfamiliar, but it means C minor seventh flat five. It is a half-diminished seventh chord.

◇ A few measures later, there is another strange-looking symbol. There is a D-flat minor chord in measure 28 notated with this: $^{(ma7)}$. This creates a minor triad with a major seventh.

◇ Another notable symbol on this lead sheet is A♭/C. The A-flat symbol indicates an A-flat major triad. And the /C indicates that the chord is inverted and the lowest-sounding note of the harmony should be a C, not the root A-flat.

QUESTIONS TO CONSIDER

1 What is a lead sheet, and how is it different from traditional music notation?

2 How does a musician interpret a lead sheet and create a performance?

TEA FOR TWO

VINCENT YOUMANS

Applying Music Theory to Great Music

The video component of this lesson is a final exam of sorts. It is based on Clara Schumann's Three Romances for Violin and Piano. This guidebook chapter provides the score for all three movements, the questions posed by the course's instructor in the video lesson, and the answers to those questions. The lesson is broken up by movement. (Note that the bonus questions at the end of the lesson cover material from the entire course.)

Three Romances

for Violin and Piano

Clara Schumann

Movement 1

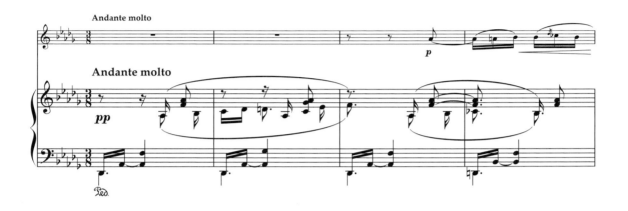

Questions and Answers from Movement 1

◇ The first movement presents some interesting challenges, especially around the modulation to a new key.

QUESTIONS

1   What key is the first movement of Three Romances for Violin and Piano?

2   Is the meter simple or compound?

3   Where does the first phrase of this piece end?

4   What is an authentic cadence?

5   What is an accidental?

6   A G dominant seventh chord moving to a C minor triad is what kind of cadence?

7   What is a crescendo?

8   What is the relative minor key of D-flat major?

9   What does the music that begins in measure 49 sound like?

ANSWERS

1 The first movement is in the key of D-flat major.

2 Simple.

3 Measure 11.

4 Motion from a dominant harmony to a tonic harmony at the end of a phrase. The harmonic motion from an A-flat dominant seventh chord to a D-flat tonic triad is a clear example of an authentic cadence in the key of D-flat major.

5 A sharp or flat in front of a note that often negates the key signature.

6 An authentic cadence.

7 An increase in dynamics over a period of time.

8 B-flat minor. A consistent use of A naturals helps to suggest B-flat minor instead of D-flat major.

9 The very beginning of the movement.

Movement 2

Questions and Answers from Movement 2

◇ The second movement's questions focus on the spelling of chords and harmonies. When listening to this movement, which begins in the key of G minor, be on the lookout for phrases that end unexpectedly.

QUESTIONS

1 What is the key signature for G minor?

2 What value note gets the beat in $\frac{2}{4}$?

3 What are the notes of a D major triad?

4 What are the notes of an E-flat major triad?

5 What is the name of an E-flat major triad in the key of G minor?

6 What is the key signature for G major?

7 What are the notes of a D dominant seventh chord?

8 What is the difference between a G minor triad and G major triad?

LESSON 18—APPLYING MUSIC THEORY TO GREAT MUSIC

ANSWERS

1 Two flats.

2 The quarter note.

3 D, F-sharp, and A.

4 E-flat, G, and B-flat.

5 Submediant.

6 One sharp.

7 D, F-sharp, A, and C.

8 The G minor triad has an F natural, and the G major triad has an F-sharp.

The second movement of Three Romances for Violin and Piano begins in G minor; however, it ends not with a G minor triad but instead with a G major triad. When a piece written in a minor key ends with a major harmony, this is known as a Picardy third. A Picardy third specifically refers to the third of the triad, which in this case was an F-sharp instead of an F natural.

The name Picardy comes from an 18th-century music dictionary written by Jean-Jacques Rousseau. Though he was likely referring to the Picardy region of France, the reason why is unknown.

Movement 3

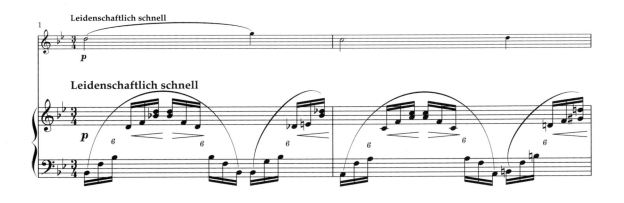

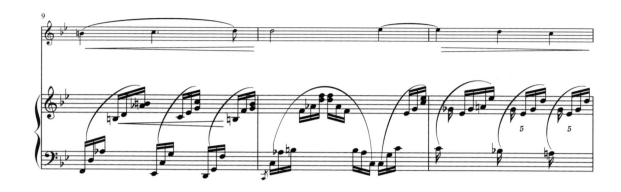

Questions and Answers from Movement 3

◇ The final movement of the Three Romances begins not in G minor but in B-flat major. The most striking difference between this movement and the first two movements is the texture: The third movement's piano-generated texture is much more fluid. But like the other two movements, this movement also modulates to a new key in the middle section, and it ultimately returns to the original key with the original themes.

QUESTIONS

1 What are the notes of an F major triad?

2 What are dynamics in music?

3 Starting in measure 42, where is the next cadence?

4 What is a musical sentence?

ANSWERS

1 F, A, and C.

2 The loudness or softness of a piece of music.

3 The next cadence is a half cadence in measure 49.

4 A phrase of music that features two short ideas followed by a longer, concluding idea.

Bonus Questions and Answers

◇ These questions cover material from the entire course. Answers follow on page 110.

QUESTIONS

1 True or False: A treble clef would be used to write music for a tuba.

2 What is the relative minor key of A major?

    a F minor

    b F-sharp minor

    c C minor

    d A minor

3 Which of the following is the correct pattern of whole steps (W) and half steps (H) in a major scale?

    a W-H-W-H-W-W-W

    b H-W-W-W-H-W-W

    c W-W-H-W-W-W-H

    d W-W-H-H-W-W-W

4 True or False: A minor third interval is bigger than a major second interval.

5 Which major key has three sharps in its key signature?

    a G major

    b C major

    c E major

    d A major

6 The meter signature of $\frac{6}{8}$ indicates that there are how many beats in each measure?

    a 2

    b 3

    c 6

    d 8

7 The symbol **C** at the beginning of a piece of music stands for common time and indicates which of the following meter signatures?

    a $\frac{3}{4}$

    b $\frac{4}{4}$

    c $\frac{2}{4}$

    d $\frac{9}{8}$

8 What is the correct spelling of a D minor triad?

    a D, F, A

    b D, F-sharp, A

    c D, F, A-flat

    d D, F, A-sharp

9 True or False: The Italian term *piano* indicates that the music should be played slowly.

10 Which of the following terms means fast?

    a *Lento*

    b *Adagio*

    c *Allegro*

    d *Maestoso*

11 The leading tone almost always wants to resolve to what note?

    a The dominant

    b The tonic

    c The mediant

    d The subdominant

12 What is the correct spelling of a G dominant seventh chord?

   a G, B-flat, D-flat, F

   b G, B, D, F-sharp

   c G, B, D-flat, F

   d G, B, D, F

13 In the key of F major, how does the C major triad function?

   a Tonic

   b Pre-dominant

   c Dominant

14 The term *staccato* means what?

   a Short and separated

   b Long and connected

   c Heavily accented

   d Moderate tempo

15 True or False: An authentic cadence is motion from a dominant harmony to a tonic harmony at a moment of rest in the music.

16 On a lead sheet, what chord is represented by the symbol F^7?

    a   F major seventh chord

    b   F dominant seventh chord

    c   F minor seventh chord

    d   F major triad

17 Which of the following is not true about the meter signature of $\frac{3}{4}$?

    a   It contains three beats per measure.

    b   It is a simple meter.

    c   The eighth note gets the beat.

    d   The quarter note gets the beat.

18 What is syncopation?

    a   Rhythms that emphasize the off-beats

    b   Gradually increasing the dynamics over time

    c   Slowing down

    d   Playing forcefully

19 What is the key signature for D-flat major?

    a 2 flats

    b 5 flats

    c 4 flats

    d 3 flats

20 True or False: Parallel octaves and fifths are not allowed when composing using counterpoint.

21 In the key of D major, what is the submediant triad?

    a F-sharp minor triad

    b G major triad

    c A major triad

    d B minor triad

22 Tonic harmonies move to pre-dominant harmonies, which then move to which type of harmony?

    a Mediant

    b Dominant

    c Subdominant

    d Submediant

23 True or False: A period in music consists of two phrases in which the first phrase ends with an authentic cadence and the second phrase ends with a half cadence.

24 What is the most common hypermeter grouping in music?

    a 4

    b 5

    c 2

    d 3

ANSWERS

1 F; **2** B; **3** C; **4** T; **5** D; **6** A; **7** B; **8** A; **9** F; **10** C; **11** B; **12** D; **13** C; **14** A; **15** T; **16** B; **17** C; **18** A; **19** B; **20** T; **21** D; **22** B; **23** F; **24** A

Russian Easter Overture

Nikolai Rimsky-Korsakov

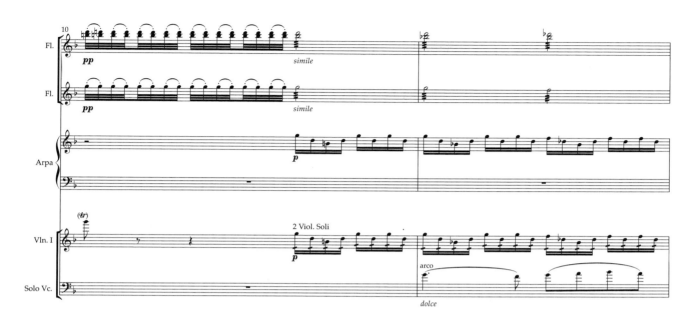

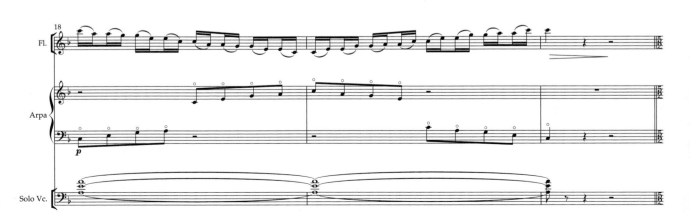

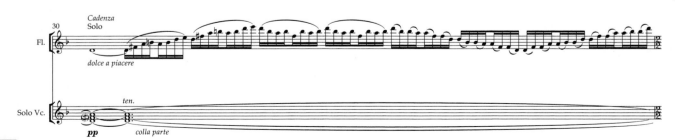

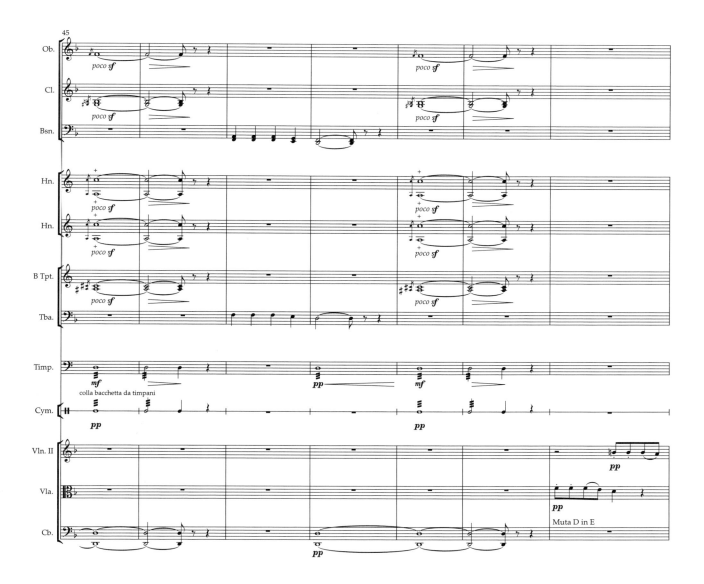

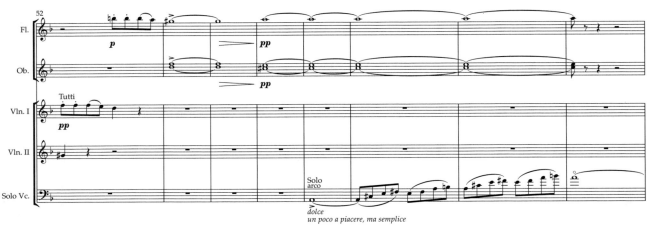

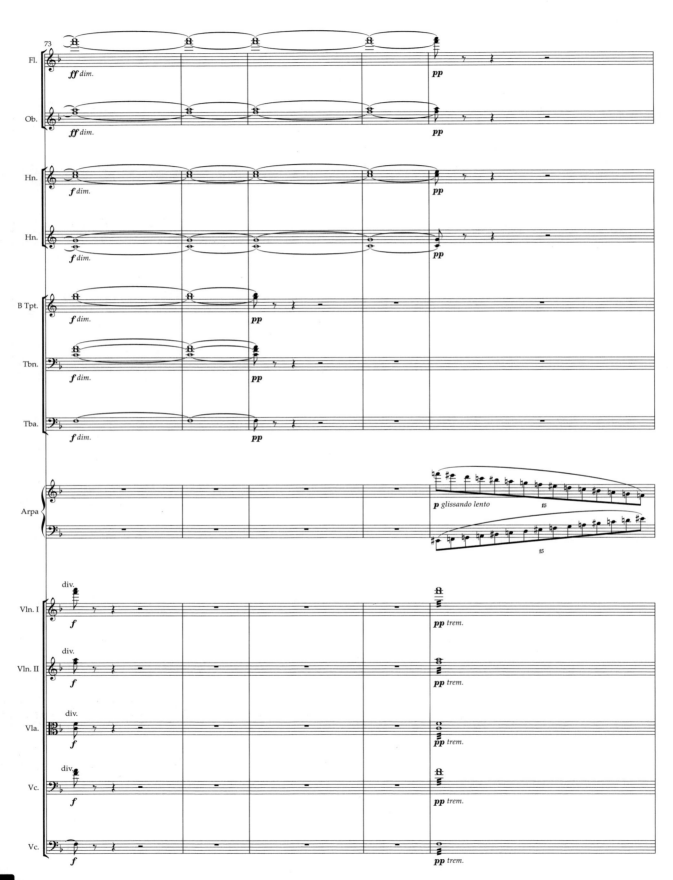

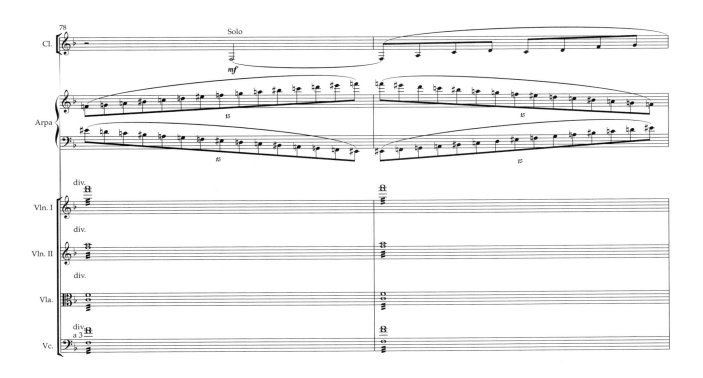

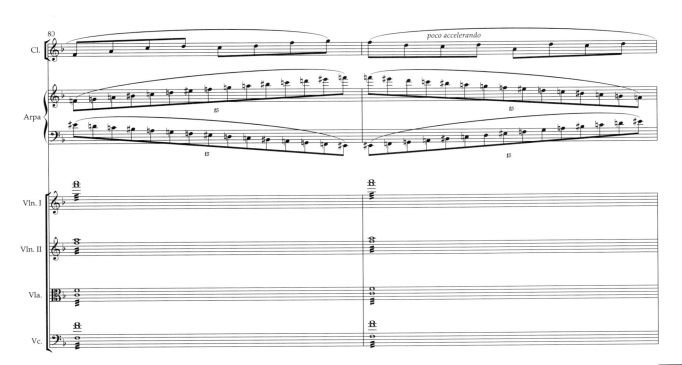

131

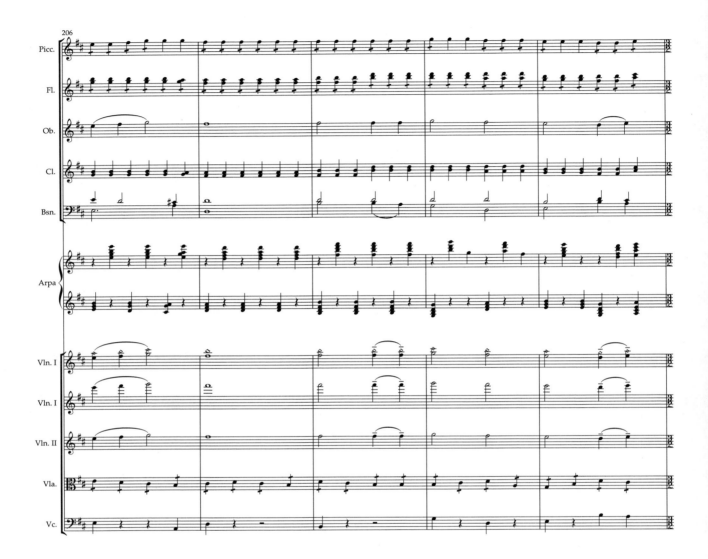

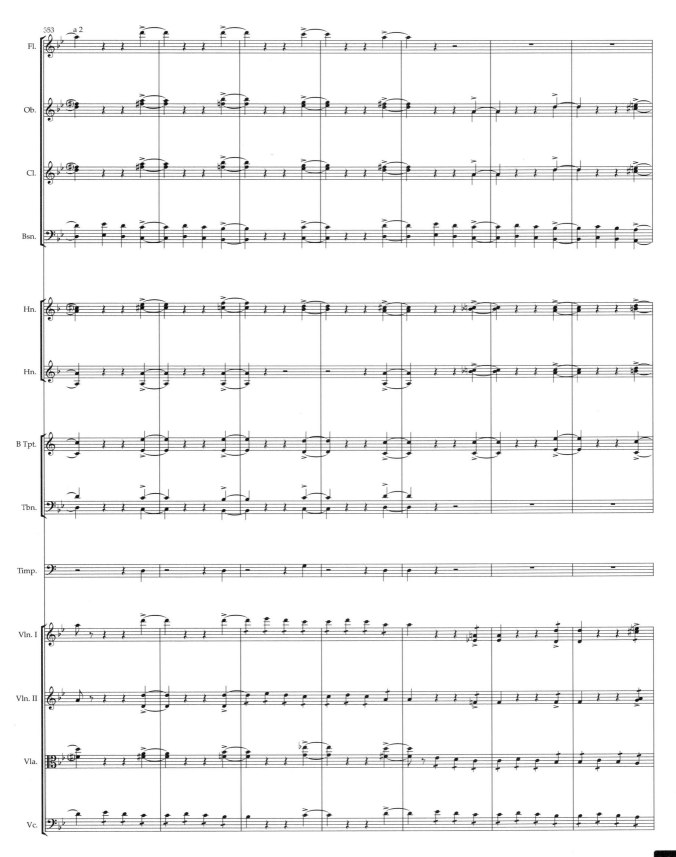

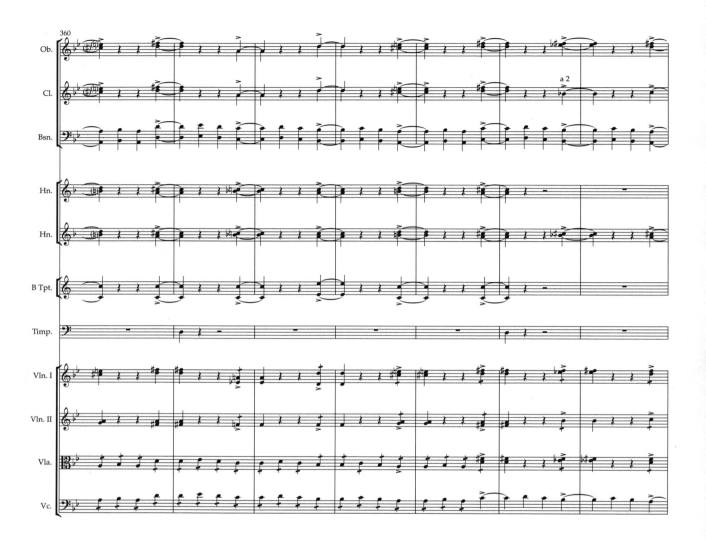

181

211

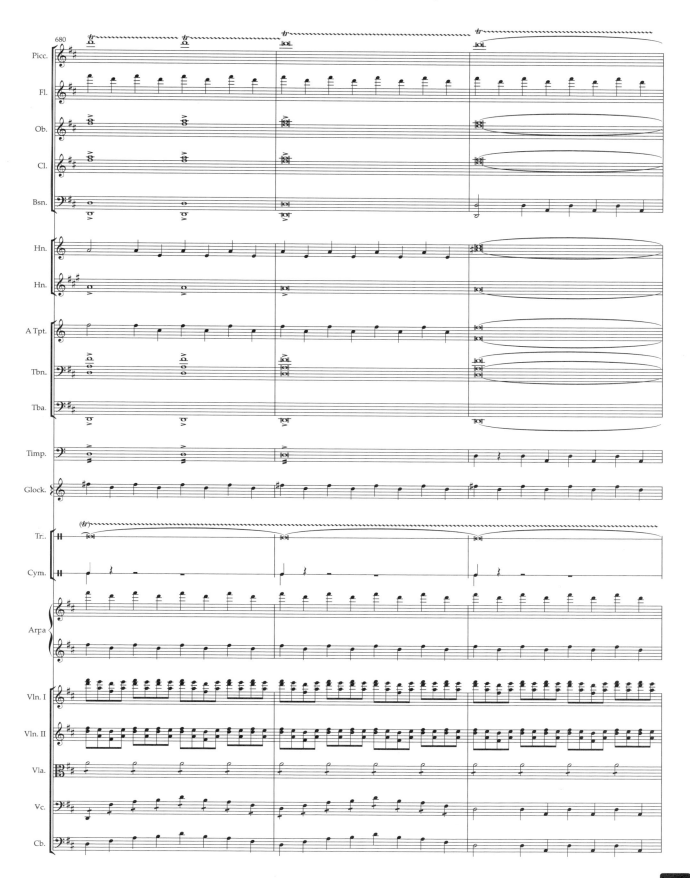

Bibliography

Burkholder, J. Peter, Donald Jay Grout, and Claude V. Palisca. *A History of Western Music*. 10th ed. New York: W.W. Norton, Inc., 2019.

Collins, Jacob, Allison King, and Andrew Moenning. Program notes for "Clara Schumann Bicentennial Celebration (1819–2019)." Fort Worth, PepsiCo Recital Hall, September 13, 2019.

Feder, Georg, and James Webster. "Haydn, (Franz) Joseph." In *Grove Music Online*. 2001. https://doi.org/10.1093/gmo/9781561592630.article.44593.

Fux, Johann Joseph. *Gradus ad Parnassum*. Translated by Alfred Mann. New York: W.W. Norton, 1965.

Hoffman, Richard, William Pelto, and John W. White. "Takadimi: A Beat-Oriented System of Rhythm Pedagogy." *Journal of Music Theory Pedagogy* 10 (1996): 7–30. https://jmtp.appstate.edu/takadimi-beat-oriented-system-rhythm-pedagogy.

Hung, Yu-Hsien Judy. "The Violin Sonata of Amy Beach." PhD diss., Louisiana State University, 2005. https://digitalcommons.lsu.edu/gradschool_dissertations/864/.

Huscher, Phillip. "Nikolai Rimsky-Korsakov—Russian Easter Overture, Op. 36." Program notes for Rimsky-Korsakov's Russian Easter Overture. The Chicago Symphony Orchestra. https://cso.org/uploadedfiles/1_tickets_and_events/program_notes/programnotes_rimskykorsakov_russianeaster.pdf.

Music Theory Examples by Women. "Clara Schumann (1818–1886)." Accessed May 17, 2020. https://musictheoryexamplesbywomen.com/composers/clara-schumann-1818-1886/.

Reich, Nancy B. "Schumann [née Wieck], Clara." In *Grove Music Online*. 2001. https://doi.org/10.1093/gmo/9781561592630.article.25152.

Semjen, Andras, Dirk Vorberg, and Han-Henning Schulze. "Getting Synchronized with the metronome: Comparisons between Phase and Period Correction." *Psychological Research* 61 (1998): 44–55. https://doi.org/10.1007/s004260050012.

Yeo, Douglas. "Le Monde du Serpent." Accessed June 3, 2020. http://www.yeodoug.com/publications/le_monde_du_serpent/le_monde_du_serpent_notes.html.

IMAGE CREDITS

Score excerpts transcribed by Emily Horton and Sean Atkinson.